Banking in Rural Areas and Agricultural Development
A Regional Perspective

Banking in Rural Areas and Agricultural Development

A Regional Perspective

K. Sivachithappa
T.D.Thimmaiya

ADHYAYAN

ADHYAYAN PUBLISHERS & DISTRIBUTORS
New Delhi-110002

Published by
ADHYAYAN PUBLISHERS & DISTRIBUTORS
4378/4B, 105, J.M.D. House, Murari Lal Street
Ansari Road Darya Ganj, New Delhi - 110002
Ph.: 011-23263018, 011-23277156, Fax: 23280028
Email: adhyayanpublishers@yahoo.com

Banking in Rural Areas and Agricultural Development
A Regional Perspective

Edition 2010
ISBN 978-81-8435-246-7

Printed in India

Published by Harish Chandra Yadav for Adhyayan Publishers & Distributors, Delhi. Laser Typesetting at Jain Computers and Printed at Tarun Offset Printers, Delhi

Preface

The book entitled "Banking in Rural Areas and Agricultural Development - A Regional Perspective" is purely a research study conducted in Mysore district of Karnataka State. India continues to be primarily a rural India with nearly 70% of its population seeking employment and living in the rural sector. Since the rural people were unable to meet their credit requirements from their own sources there was a need for providing timely and adequate institutional credit to small, marginal farmers. Thus the Regional Rural Banks came into existence. The small and marginal farmers and rural artisans find it difficult to make investment on modern inputs like high yielding varieties of seeds chemical fertilizers, purchase of raw materials and improved machinery as they do not have sufficient funds of their own for investment purpose. Hence Grameena Banks have to extend credit for investment.

Majority of the rural fold especially weaker sections of the society including small farmers are not able to meet their day-to-day requirements from their own sources of income not to speak of investigating in other productive enterprises for improving their economic conditions. Therefore, they have to depend on various financial agencies for getting funds for making investment. To bring about the overall development in the rural areas, financial assistance (especially regional rural banks assistance) to the rural poor needs emphasis.

Hence, it is high time to make an empirical evaluation

of the various regional rural banks schemes, aimed at generation of additional employment and income, and thus alleviation of the rural poverty, so that the various lacunae could be made more meaningful and be strengthened in the light of experience. In this juncture, we have conducted a research survey in Mysore district to evaluate the role of Cauvery Grameena Bank in agricultural development. This study is more helpful to academicians, researchers, policy makers and general readers.

We would like to thank the proprietor of Adhyayan Publishers and Distributors, New Delhi for his cooperation in bringing out the book.

We are grateful to God for this inspiration and effort, which we hope, will satisfy the inquisitiveness of young budding researchers.

K. Sivachithappa
T.D.Thimmaiya

List of Tables

Abbreviations

BPL	-	Below Poverty Line
CGB	-	Cauvery Grameena Bank
DCCBs	-	District Central Cooperative Banks
DES	-	Department of Economics and Statistics
DRI	-	Differential Rate of Interest
DSO	-	District Statistical Office
GoI	-	Government of India
HYVP	-	High Yielding Variety Programme
ISEC	-	Institute for Social and Economic Change
KCC	-	Kisan Credit Card
NABARD	-	National Bank for Agriculture and Rural Development
NGB	-	Netravathi Grameena Bank
NGO	-	Non-Governmental Organisations
NIRD	-	National Institute of Rural Development
PACS	-	Primary Agricultural Credit Societies
RBI	-	Reserve Bank of India
RKBY	-	Rastriya Krishi Bima Yojana
RRBs	-	Regional Rural Banks

SACP	-	Special Agricultural Credit Plans
SCBs	-	State Cooperative Banks
SGB	-	Sahyadri Grameena Bank
SHG	-	Self-Help Group
SLBC	-	State Level Bankers Committee
TGB	-	Thungabhadra Grameena Bank
WDC	-	Women Development Cell

Contents

1

Introduction

The Setting

Rural development remains an uphill task due to the complexity of problems existing in the rural sector. The rural sector requires a multi-dimensional approach to reach cost-effective solutions to these problems. The rural areas suffer from poor infrastructural facilities. The villages are yet to emerge as the main centres of production activity. The productivity is to produce goods in urban areas, even to meet the basic needs of rural consumers. This apart, the rural population requires not one but a few inputs and services. These have to be provided at the right time and in the right sequence. This demands the right kind of co-ordination amongst agencies extending help to the rural sector.[1]

Rural economy is weaker sector of the national economy and even in the rural economy, a major segment is not only weak but in a miserable state. Regional Rural Banks (RRBs) seem to be the only hope in injects strength and accelerate the growth of rural economy and ensure the development of rural areas. Rural development in India is recognized as a sine qua non for faster economic development and welfare of common masses. Rural development is not merely development of rural areas but also the development of the rural peoples into self-reliant and self-sustaining modern little communities. Rural development is, therefore the development of rural areas in such a way that each component of rural life changes in a desired direction and in sympathy with the other components.[2]

In Indian economy rural sector plays a significant role. It affects directly or indirectly almost all the economic activities in the country. It employs the maximum number of people. It is also the most important source of national income in India. It also supplies food for the survival of the entire population of India. It also supplies materials necessary for the major industries of India. A large part of the revenue of the Government is also obtained from rural sector. In short, rural sector can be rightly considered as the backbone of our economy. In spite of the significant role of the rural sector, it continues to be neglected. The magnitude of poverty, illiteracy, and ill health is of higher order in the rural areas as compared to the urban areas.

The rural sector requires institutional credit to take up economically viable projects. But it needs to be noted that credit alone cannot deliver the goods. There is what is called the credit absorption capacity of the region. This depends on the implementation of economically viable schemes. Hence, the formulation of economic plans should precede the preparation of credit plans. There are certain agencies like the co-operatives, regional rural banks and farmers service societies which are most appropriate to serve the rural population, but their performance needs to be toned up. Of course, cheap credit needs to be discouraged.

Majority of the rural fold are not able to meet their day-to-day requirements from their own sources of income not to speak of investigating in other productive enterprises for improving their economic conditions. Therefore, they have to depend on various financial agencies for getting funds for making investment. To bring about the overall development in the rural areas, financial assistance to the rural poor, particularly institutional assistance for the development of agriculture needs no emphasis. Finance is an essential requirement for almost every activity. If required finance is not available out of ones own income then one needs credit. In rural areas of India, credit requirements are more pressing. Rural credit in India is a part and parcel of its economic development. Rural population is composed of agricultural producers, tenant cultivators, village artisans and landless labour. All these categories are in need of credit. To provide the credit requirements to these categories regional rural banks play very significant role.[3]

It is felt that, the era of economic liberalization has broadly circumvented the RRBs to a large extent. Though, some initiatives were taken for RRBs in terms of freedom in interest rate structure, relaxation in target group concept, parity of emoluments to staff with sponsor bank, etc., albeit these interventions have been inadequate, delayed and tentative. As cardinal changes are contemplated in the rural credit delivery system in near future, it is indispensable to synchronize the operations of RRB with the challenges ahead. The opportunities, threats, etc., are to be perceived in context of rapid refinements taking place on financial horizons and there is fundamental necessity for carrying out reforms in RRBs to overcome their limitations. RRBs today face number of impediments in their holistic growth. The foremost being the pro poor (rural/poor man's bank) image of RRBs. Public still perceives these banks as 'only for poor or rural people.[4]

The Need of Agricultural Credit in India

The credit is a basic input for any development programme. This is particularly true for agricultural development, which has its goal to improve the standards of living of realties as well as to increase agricultural productivity. Unless sufficient credit is provided to the development programme for the weaker section of the society the goal of development programmes cannot be achieved[5].

The credit requirements of the Indian farmers can be classified into three types depending upon the period and the purpose for which they are required.

1. Reserve Bank of India classified credit needs of the agriculturist into following purposes.
   (a) Credit is needed for the purchase of seed, manure and fodder; irrigation of crops, hire charges pumps and purchase of water purchase of livestock and effecting other land improvements and construction of irrigation wells and tanks and other capital expenditure on agriculture.
   (b) Credit is needed for production and transport equipment.
   (c) Credit is needed for paying for medical, educational expenses, purchase or construction and repair of residential houses.
2. Loans contracted by farmers can also be classified on the basis of time into three categories.
   (a) Agriculturist needs credit for short periods a less than 15 months for the purpose of cultivation or for meeting domestic expenses for example they want to buy seeds, fertilizers fodder for cattle, etc. Such short-period loans are normally repaid after the harvest.
   (b) The farmers require finance for medium period ranging between 15 months and 5 years for the purpose of making some improvement on land buying cattle, agricultural implements.
   (c) The farmers need finances for the purpose of buying additional land to make permanent improvements on land and purchase costly agricultural machinery.

Productive and Unproductive Credit Needs

The credit requirements of farmers can be classified into

two types—productive and unproductive loans. The farmer includes loans to buy seeds, fertilizers, implements, etc. To pay taxes to the Government and to make permanent improvements on land such as digging and deepening of wells, fencing of land. All these forms of credit help the farmers in their agricultural operations or improving their land besides these the Indian farmer borrows for unproductive purpose. Such as celebration of marriage, births and deaths.

The problem of agricultural credit is unique, in the sense that, the prospective borrowers are to be reckoned in millions, their creditworthiness is practically nil, their needs of great urgency, their knowledge of accounting matter is small, and their economic status is low. The policy-maker should aim at securing the economic and political health of the people through agricultural credit.[6]

The importance of agricultural credit in a country like India, which is essentially rural in nature hardly, needs elaboration. Economic development of the countryside hinges upon availability of credit to rural economy. The burden of indebtedness in rural India is great, and falls mainly on the households of rural working people. The exploitation of this group in the credit market is one of the most pervasive and persistent features of rural life in India.[7] Despite major structural changes in credit institutions and forms of agricultural credit in the post-independence period, Darwin's statement (1925), that "the Indian peasant is born in debt, lives in debt and bequeaths debt", still remains true for the great majority of agricultural households in the countryside. Rural households need credit for a variety of reasons.

Statement of the Problem

India continues to be primarily a rural India with nearly 70% of its population seeking employment and living in the rural sector. Since the rural people were unable to meet their credit requirements from their own sources there was a need for providing timely and adequate institutional credit to small, marginal farmers. Thus the Regional Rural Banks came into existence. The small and marginal farmers and rural artisans find it difficult to make investment on modern inputs like high yielding varieties of seeds chemical fertilizers, purchase of raw materials and improved machinery as they do not have sufficient funds of their own for investment purpose. Hence Grameena Banks have to extend credit for investment.

Majority of the rural fold especially weaker sections of the society including small farmers are not able to meet their day-to-day requirements from their own sources of income not to speak of investigating in other productive enterprises for improving their economic conditions. Therefore, they have to depend on various financial agencies for getting funds for making investment. To bring about the overall development in the rural areas, financial assistance (especially regional rural banks assistance) to the rural poor needs emphasis.

Hence, it is high time to make an empirical evaluation of the various regional rural banks schemes, aimed at generation of additional employment and income, and thus alleviation of the rural poverty, so that the various lacunae could be made more meaningful and be strengthened in the light of experience.

Need for the Present Study

Regional Rural Banks main objective is to provide credit and other facilities especially to the small and marginal formers, agricultural labourers and other under privileged people in the rural areas through the generation of income and employment opportunities, Cauvery Grameena Bank was set-up in October, 2nd 1976 under Regional Rural Banks Act 1976. The primary objective of the Bank is to provide financial assistance to the priority sector such as small and marginal formers, landless labourers, tenant formers, share croppers, scheduled caste, scheduled tribes, rural artisans, petty shop keepers, and self-employed persons. This study is an attempt at evaluating the performance of Cauvery Grameena Bank in terms of branch expansion, deposit mobilization, recovery performance and utilization of credit provided to the agriculture sector. Cauvery Grameena Bank was set-up in 1976. The Bank has completed 30 years of purposeful existence; it is the right time to evaluate in depth the working and performance of Bank, in meeting the credit needs of the agricultural sector.

Objectives of the Study

It is generally felt that there have been perceptible changes in the living conditions of the farmers mainly on economic side and relatively on social side owing to the role of rural banks. This calls for a well considered strategy for prioritised basic research. It is with this perceptional background that the detailed study has been undertaken to find out the economic impact of institutional credit on the agricultural development. Impact assessment in this context implies questions about outreach and effectiveness in meeting development objectives. In the light of this, the following are the main objectives of the study:

1. To study the progress of Regional Rural Banks in India.
2. To examine the origin and growth of RRBs in the state of Karnataka.
3. To study the role of Regional Rural Banks in agricultural development.
4. To assess the effectiveness of various schemes adopted by the Cauvery Grameena Bank for the development of farming community in Mysore district.
5. To make suitable policy recommendations on the basis of findings, for the further effective working of the RRBs for the agricultural development of the region.

Hypotheses Framed in the Study

The following hypotheses have been framed for the study:

1. There is a positive correlation between Regional Rural Banks credit and development of agricultural sector.
2. Cauvery Grameena Bank sponsored programmes have helped in the development of small farmers in the district.
3. Standard of living of the beneficiaries has been improved during post-loan period.

Research Methodology and Sources of Data

The present study is based on simple random sampling method. Hence, the study is depending up on both secondary and primary data. The secondary data are collected from various publications of NABARD and Reserve Bank of India, Government of India, Department of Economics and Statistics, Karnataka, State Level Bankers Committee, Bangalore, Cauvery Grameena Bank, District Statistical Office, Mysore District. Some unpublished data are also collected from the above institutions at the district level. Data are also collected from books, periodicals and journals.

The different sources of information for the study are following:

1. *Interviews with Respondents:* The major source of information for the study was the personal interviews of the borrowers with a pre-tested comprehensive schedule. The schedule was structured to cover information pertaining to family particulars, bank loans, economics of activities financed, and levels of living of the borrowers. Information relating to the periods before and after the loans was collected from the 250 borrowers selected for the study.
2. *Bank Records:* Bank's records pertaining to the selected activities and the selected borrowers at the branches were also persuading to collect the necessary information on sanction, disbursal, and repayment etc., of the loans.

Sampling Design

Following is the sampling design of the study

Mysore District

Selected Respondents

1. Crop – 50
2. Tractor – 50
3. Digging Wells – 50
4. Dairy – 50
5. Bullock Carts – 50

Total : 250 Respondents

Reference Period for the Study

The primary data for the study have been collected from the sample beneficiaries for two time periods viz., pre-loan period, referring to the period of 2007-08 immediately preceding the sanction of loans and post-loan period referring to the year which ended on the March 2009. The secondary data for the study have been collected from the year 1997-98 to 2007-08.

Limitations of the Study

The present study pertains to only a particular district, that is Mysore district. As such the study is region specific and generalizations are too limited to other districts of the state. Further, it should be pointed out that non-institutional finance still owns up an important share in the credit advanced to agriculture sector by the regional rural banks. The present study limits itself only to the analysis of regional rural banks credit which itself forms a limitation.

Chapter Scheme of the Study

The study consist of six chapters, following is the chapter scheme of the study:

Chapter – 1

Introduction

The first chapter deals with introduction of the study, its objectives, need for the study, statement of the problem and methodology adopted for the study, hypotheses and sample design of the study. This chapter serves as the foundation on the basis of which the other chapters of the study are developed.

Chapter – 2

Review of Literature

The second chapter deals with review of the previous studies concerned to subject-matter. In this chapter, a brief review of research studies conducted by individual researchers and research institutions on agriculture sector and institutional credit in India and also in Karnataka State, finally research gaps are also identified.

Chapter – 3

Growth of Regional Rural Banks in India – An Overview

Third chapter is on the growth and performance of Regional Rural Banks in India, it gives an overview of the branch expansion, deposit mobilization and agricultural credit performance of the regional rural banks.

Chapter – 4

Performance of Regional Rural Banks in Karnataka – An Analysis

This chapter covers, performance evaluation of the regional rural banks in Karnataka, in terms of branch expansion, deposit mobilization, agricultural credit, etc.

Chapter – 5

Regional Rural Banks and Agricultural Development in Mysore District — Case Study Analysis

Chapter fifth deals with socio-economic profile of the study area – Mysore district, covering geographical conditions, occupational structure, and banking activities and performance of Cauvery Grameen Bank in Mysore district and its financial assistance to various sectors in the district economy. The case study analysis has been presented in this chapter. Hence this chapter is considered as core chapter of the study.

Chapter – 6

Summary, Major Findings and Policy Implications

The last chapter sets out a summary and presents the conclusions of the study. It also attempts the suggestions about the better performance of regional rural banks in general and Cauvery Grameena Bank in particular.

References

1. Srinivasan, G. (2002): *Focus on Rural Infrastructure and Poverty Alleviation Programmes,* Kurukshetra, Vol.50, No.6, April 2002.
2. Bankimchandra, V.Vaidya (2002): *Some Aspects of Rural Development,* Kurukshetra, Vol. 50, No. 6, April 2002.
3. Sanjib Kumar Hota and Vinod Sharma (2001). *Cooperative Credit: Revamping Needed,* Yojana Vol. 45, July 2001.
4. *Ibid.*
5. Balishter and Roshan Singh (2001): *Rural Development and Cooperatives,* Yojana Vol. 45, July 2001.
6. Sasi Rekha, K.N and J.Rani Ratna Prabha (2008): *Agricultural Credit in India in Pre- and Post-reform Period,* Southern Economist, Vol.47, No.12, October 2008.
7. Deshpande, R.S. and Nagesh Prabhu (2005): "Farmers Distress" *Economic and Political Weekly,* October 29, pp. 4663-4665.

2

Review of Literature

This chapter deals with review of previous studies regarding RRBs and various aspects of institutional credit. In order to create a foundation for the study, to understand the various nuances and dimensions of the topic of study as well as to prepare a proper methodology and framework for the study, elaborate efforts have been made to review the available literature on the topic. Some of the significant theoretical and empirical review of literature and their points of view are presented here below:

Theoretical Studies

There are in a broad sense, both micro- and macro-economic foundations of the theory of institutional economics. The theory of institutional economics is an important part of theoretical welfare economics.

The theoretical arguments regarding the role of finance in poverty alleviation are broadly classified into two main views, the 'Development School' (Lipton, 1998). The Development School views that lack of credit is a major constraint in taking up productive activities. It believes that there is a need to steer rural credit into productive projects and into the hands of the rural poor. Ragner Nurks argues that the underdeveloped countries are plagued with vicious circle of poverty due to low productivity, low income, low saving capacity and vice-versa. Similarly, Arthur Lewis in his "Theory of Economic Growth" (1995) argues that the poor in rural areas need much more capital than they save in order to invest in productive activities. This excess in demand of capital can be met with the help of loans. Providing credit (loans) to the rural poor to meet the legitimate needs and expand their opportunities in the prime requirement.

The Development School came in for a lot of criticisms by the scholars belonging to the 'Banking School'. Profound scholars belonging to Banking School like Dale Adams, Van Pischke, Douglas Graham, Gordon Donald argue that credit does not play a leading role but a facilitating role in the process of economic development. Some of the problems that the scholars identified with the traditional credit model are, limited out reach of credit failure of the credit institutions to sustain themselves financially.

Thus, rural credit policies in low developed countries are not supportive to increase productivity in addition to reducing poverty. The decades of 50s and 60s were marked with the supply of credit, which were seen as important constraints for economic development by many developing countries. Thus, it was widely believed that providing accessibility to credit to the rural poor was considered essential to alleviate poverty and promote economic development. Although informal credit markets operated widely in rural areas, high interest rates of money-lenders hindered the process of investing in productive income activities by the rural poor (Von Pischke, 1983).

The National Government, Donors, Multilateral Financial Agencies funded credit programmes for the rural poor through various financial institutions at subsidized rates (Padmanaban, 1988). The subsidized credit lending discourages the underprivileged from saving as they provided low rate of interest (Von Pischke, 1992). The low rate of interest in the rural credit market leads to excess demand for loanable funds.

Excess demand for credit caused credit rationing by the lenders. The subsidized credit to the rural poor in developing countries did not result in the desired goal of poverty reduction. Government subsidized credits were labelled as credits that hardly reached the poor, generated economic rents, in efficiencies and financially unsustainable. In general, the past performance of the state or donor sponsored rural finance operation has fallen short of expectations.

The Conventicnal (subsidized) Credit Model was subjected to serious criticism from the mid-1970s as donor and multilateral agencies switched their attention from 'state intervention' to 'market oriented' solution. Changes in interest rate, policies and saving mobilization became the cornerstone of new thinking regarding rural financial markets.

The break down of the system gave rise to new awareness among the economists, policy-makers and donors in order to look beyond the present credit model and take on a board about the need of institutional viability and efficient allocation of resources. Thus, the Banking School Model emerged as an alternative to the traditional.

Credit Model

Mellor and Desai (1993) proposed the 'structuralism view' by stating that inappropriate organizational structure of financial institutions was a major reason for poor performance. Generally, financial institutions provide that of 'credit alone' services, which have not contributed to economic development in general and poverty alleviation in particular. This view prompted the 'credit plus' approach in development banking and led to the promotion of Multifunctional Financial Institutions which were encouraged to provide credit along with non-credit services to the poor.

Hoff and Stiglitz (1990) and their followers were instrumental in presenting what is known as the 'Information Paradigm'. This paradigm primarily emphasized the problem of information asymmetry in the rural credit market. This asymmetry characterized by three interrelated situations, viz., adverse selection, moral hazard and enforcement. Operation of these mechanisms cause rationed credit and segmented credit markets.

The group based lending which is practiced in Micro Finance Institutions can overcome fundamental barriers of financial intermediation between lenders and borrowers. The reduction of transaction cost for both the lenders and borrowers has the potential to lower these barriers there by increasing credit services to the poor in a more sustainable manner (Von Pischke at 1983, Hulme and Hosby, 1996). The success of Micro-Finance Institutions like the Grameena Bank, Bancosol of Bolivia, the BRAC and Indonesia, the SEWA in India and many others have been attributed these innovations in the provision of financial services. The institutional innovations have lowered the cost and risks of making loans to the poor due to social collateral, savings promotion and ensuring sustainability.

Empirical Studies

The empirical studies are applied research studies. They help us to test the theories or models and also provide insights to reformulate old theories and models and/or formulate new theories and models.

Arvinder Singh Chawla (1986)[1] has studied banking developments in Patiala district with special reference to branch expansion, deposit mobilization, credit deployment, priority sector lending and poverty alleviation programmes. It is concluded that, although imbalance in banking presence continues to exist, a clear trend in reduction of inter-block disparities is observed. The analysis reveals that only four banks operating in the district, which have regional character, have opened more branches in rural areas than in urban areas. All other banks have concentrated either in Urban or in Semi-Urban areas.

Bank of India (1975)[2] studied the impact of its direct financing activities in Sholapur district by comparing net farm incomes, yields, intensity of cropping and the per acre income of farmer - borrowers during the investment and post-investment periods of short-term and medium-term credit. The results indicated that the area under irrigation in the district increased by 252 acres with the bank finance. This resulted in an increase in cropping intensity employment and net income. Which was much higher on borrowers, farmers than on those of non-borrowers. The farmers who have borrowed composite loans (short-medium and long-term loans together) obtained higher incremental income than those who had borrowed crop loans only. The results also revealed that poor farmers realised higher incremental income that rich farmers.

Wadhwa[3] has made a noteworthy study, entitled "Rural Banks for Rural Development (1980)". This study covered an analysis of the progress made by all Regional Rural Banks in India and offered valuable suggestions for its restructure. This study was conducted in 1977 when the Regional Rural Banks were in the initial stages; and the assessment of their performance was premature.

Satya Sai (1986)[4] in his study of institutional credit to agriculture in west Godhavari district of Andhra Pradesh found that on average 90% of the institutional credit was utilized for productive purpose. However, a positive relationship was found between the proportion of loan amount used for productive purpose and land size similarly. Ramaswamy and Meskal (1988) in their study on commercial banks found that lending to agriculture in Coimbatore district of Tamil Nadu, found mis-utilisation of loan to extent of 38% by agricultural labour households and 20% by small farmers. Patel (1989) in his study on recovery performance of direct agricultural advances of commercial banks observed that 21% of the borrowers have diverted the bank loan for consumption requirements and 13.2% for repayment of old debts.

Shylendra (1992)[5] analyzed the economic impact of Regional Rural Banks in Karnataka (RRBs - TGB) loans. The utilisation pattern showed that under none of the purposes of the borrowing, the loan has been used to the full extent of sanction for the intended purpose, he found that borrowers has diverted 4 to 24% of the loan amount from intended purpose to other uses. However, the borrowers were found to be using major share of their loans (about 89%) to various productive purposes.

Rai *et al.* (1975)[6] studied the role of institutional credit in Kalyanapur block of Kanpur district, Uttar Pradesh and found that the cropping intensity on the borrowers and non-borrower farms was 170.4 and 145.4% respectively. The area under high yielding varieties was about 68.91 and 20.93% on borrowers and non-borrowers farms in that order. The per hectare overall input-output ratio net income family labour income and farm business income for the borrowers farms were higher when compared with the non-borrower farms. The ratio of additional cost on account of institutional credit and income generated indicated that one rupee of credit would generate on overall income of Rs. 2.72 the highest ratio of 1:3, 0: 2 between institutional credit cost and income was seen on the larger size farm followed by the medium farm (1:267). The lowest ratio of 1:2, 5 was seen in the size groups of 0-2.5 hectares. Since these farms did not devote all they're available credit to production expenses.

Vijayakumar (1975)[7] in his study on credit requirements and its impact on irrigatedand unirrigated farms in Bangalore South Taluk used linear programming models. He found that the requirements of credit on irrigated farms were marginal, though there is a possibility to increase the net returns by 2.5% with use of improved technology. In the use of unirrigated farms provision of Rs.1005 as short-term credit in Kharif Season enabled the farmers to realize 51.5% of additional net returns over what the farmers could get without credit with improved technology crops, external financial activities in terms of long-medium and short-term loans for converting unirrigated farms into irrigated farms were found to be feasible.

Rao and Wahan (1974)[8] in their study on Agricultural finance by Commercial Banks in South Canara district of Karnataka found that the increased credit facility enabled a good number of farmers to improve their cultural practices and many borrower farmers began to grow high yielding paddy varieties in the study area. The average gross income of farmers has increased by 74% from Rs.14,890 in reference year to Rs.25,784 in current year. The per centage increase across size groups was the lowest (66.33%) for the small farmers and highest (80.69%) on the medium farmers. Along with the income, the cost of cultivation has also increased significantly over the period.

Kavarjital *et al.* (1981)[9] in their study about the impact of farm loans on farm income and employment pattern in Panagar Block of Jabalpur district found that the net farm income increased on all categories of farmers often avoiding loan, incremental income was the highest in case of small farms and more or less equal in medium and large farms. The change in hired labour employment due to borrowing of loan was observed to be the highest in case of small farmers followed by medium and large farmers.

Hanumanthaiah (1979)[10] studied the commercial banks performance in financing agriculture in the Parchuree block of Prakasham district of Andhra Pradesh. He found that the performance of commercial banks was satisfactory to finance agriculture (short-term loans) in terms of quantum of loan advance coverage of small farmers recovery of loans and the rate of interest. The results indicated that there is a scope for increasing the net farm returns by about Rs.10,902 through reallocation of resources even at the existing level of loan limits. The availability of additional funds and the consequent changes in cropping pattern would increase the labour employment in the region.

Kutty *et al.* (1974)[11] took up a study of the impact of long-term – credit on agriculture in Uthanagar taluk of Dharmapuri district of Tamilnadu. The average cost of cultivation per gross cropped areas was higher on the beneficiary farms when compared with the non-beneficiary category (due to higher use of inputs) and the same was true with regard to the gross income and gross profits. They concluded that the investment in permanent resource improvement had generated demand for additional short-term investment for purchase of inputs.

Jugale (1997) [12] inferred that the term loan for agricultural purpose granted by zonal development Bank enabled the borrowers to improve form mechanization by purchasing tractor, tillers and IP sets for minor irrigation the term loan also helped in increasing irrigated area by 22.40 per cent of landholding a well as cropping patterns and cropping intensity from one crop to two crops a year.

Veerashekarappa (1997)[13] in his study on institutional finance for rural development. Concluded that institutional finance was instrumental in acquiring productive form assets and development of irrigation facilities this results in changes in the cropping pattern increase in the cropping intensity and adoption of HYVs.

Sasi Rekha, K.N. and J. Rani Ratna Prabha (2008)[14] in the study on "Agricultural Credit in India in Pre- and Post-Reform Period" observed that the problem of agricultural credit is unique, in the sense that, the prospective borrowers are to be reckoned in millions, their creditworthiness is practically nil, their needs of great urgency, their knowledge of accounting matter is small, and their economic status is low. The policy-maker should aim at securing the economic and political health of the people through agricultural credit.

Reddy, Y.V. (2004)[15] in the study of Rural Credit: Status and Agenda" observed that the main problem to be solved in connection with Indian agricultural credit is that of providing loans for millions of uncreditworthiness are mutually irreconcilable, if agricultural credit viewed is solely as a financial matter involving only lending and repayment, a solution to the problem is unlikely to merge, it would have to be viewed in the larger perspective of the national purpose, which rural credit is intended to subserve.

Deshpande, R.S. and Nagesh Prabhu (2005) [16] in their study observed that the policy-maker should aim at securing the economic and political health of the people through agricultural credit. They should regard the principles of finance and accounting, but they should not be overemphasized. Agricultural credit is a matter which affects millions of people and in democracy, it is important that the people should also try to understand the rights and wrongs of borrowing matters which affect them. Their participation and opinion will shape the government policy.

Chandrasekhar Rao, G. (1989)[17] in his study on "How are Rural Commercial Banks" observed that inspite of all the efforts made by institutional agencies the small and marginal farmers are still depending on the informal agencies for the credit needs. This situation can find remedy when the small and marginal farmers has been provided credit with putting less margin for the viability and security and by giving less importance to the commercial viability and profitability of formal agencies.

Nanda Pandey (1989)[18] in his study on "Commercial Banks and Rural Development" has concluded that if commercial banks aim at reaching the poor peasants, rural artisans and other rural people with small or no assets or means, the banks will not only have to develop appropriate organizational skills but also change their attitudes in favour of the hitherto neglected sector of the rural economy. Opening of commercial bank branches in rural areas is often were a ritual, meant mainly to fulfil physical targets but without any firm commitment or even the faintest notion of serving rural areas and customers. It is suggested in the study that the staff position of banks should be augmented where necessary.

Deshpande (1989)[19] in his work on "reaching the poor" has noted that to enable the poor to come forward to take advantage of any scheme, we must create a cadre of local village youths who will organize the poor, train them, supervise the economic activity and, in general, guide them for their development in a comprehensive sense of the term.

Anti-poverty programme has to take into accent all these aspects if effective and lasting results are to be achieved. It is observed that provision of credit assistance is not enough. In fact, it has only second priority. It is essential to identify obstacles in the development process before any scheme is introduced to a region. The conditions differ from region to region and it may not be possible for the government to prepare a development programme for each region. The local level officials should be encouraged to make an effort to understand local conditions and make suggestions to the higher authorities.

State Bank of Patiala (1989)[20] has in its study on rural lending in Patiala district recorded that the scale of finance for crop loan is inadequate due to increased cost of inputs. The farmers are still in the clutches of money-lenders/ commission agents who are charging exorbitant interest rates, ranging from 30 to 35 per cent per annum. The commission agents bind down the farmers by making advance to them and exploit them at the time of purchase of their produce. It has been suggested that the instead of giving capital-subsidy, the beneficiaries should be provided kind subsidy, i.e., waiving off interest, insurance of animal, etc. It has been observed that shortage of staff at the branches leads to poor exploitation of resources in the form of deposits.

Singh Pasricha (1991)[21] has studied the role of bank finance in the rural development in Punjab and has reported that subsidy-linked social banking schemes should be reoriented in order to check the misutilisation of loans taken just to grab subsidy. It is suggested that subsidy should be released only when the principal amount is repaid. Moreover, the sponsoring agencies should adhere to the quarterly targets assigned to them, while sponsoring loan cases to the financing banks.

Giriyappa (1993)[22] has examined the role of agriculture, forestry and sericulture as traditional sub-sector of rural development process on the one hand and examined the income and employment effects of the impact of IRDP with reference to D.K. district, Bangalore and Kolar districts in Karnataka State on the other hand. The most important findings of their study is that small and marginal farmers, fisherman, artisans, labourers, SC and ST households and also female headed households face the problem of low-income generation and low asset formation. The assistance through the IRD programme is minimal and persists in bare subsistence.

Kaladhar (1997)[23] studied the design, structure and governance of micro-finance in India. It revealed that the outreach of the programme as have been increasing over the years through the help and assistance from SEWA, NGOs, IRDP programmes, Co-operative Banks and Commercial Banks. Banking sector reforms have tried to remove some of the imperfections, which were dealt in detail by institutional economics.

Upadhyay and Kaveri (1982)[24] in their study on "Impact of Bank Finance on the Decentralized Sector" have observed that bank funds are not fully utilized for business purpose and hence have not made any significant impact on the small business units. A majority of the borrowers use a part of the bank finance for consumption purpose. Hence, it is advisable to grant consumption loans separately apart from business. Moreover, the non-borrowers should be educated on the salient features on bank schemes, in which task bank staff has to play a vital role. It is essential to establish a rapport with them and convince them on the scope of bank schemes and the desirability of availing them.

Economic and Statistical Organization, Punjab (1983)[25] has conducted a study of commercial bank loans advanced to weaker sections of the community in Punjab. It has been observed that there is no proper scrutiny of applications by sponsoring agencies. The purpose for which loan is being asked for remains quite vague. It is also noted that the sponsoring agencies do not keep a record of the cases sponsored to the financing banks; this sometimes leads to duplication in advancing loans. It is suggested that on- the spot loaning should not be done, as it does not allow proper scrutiny of the applications.

Patel and Shete (1984)[26] have reported in their study on "weaker section loans" that banks feel nervous about the extent of overdues in weaker section financing. They have also reported the increasing overdues on the one hand, and the policy-makers expectations of the bankers to cover more and more weaker sections in the minds of general public and nervousness at the gross roots level bankers. But the researchers have found that the recovery of bank loans from DRI beneficiaries was better than that of non-DRI beneficiaries.

The State Bank of Patiala (1987)[27] has conducted a study to known the impact of bank lending in rural areas in Patiala district. The study reveals that there is proper coordination between the lead bank and government agencies but coordination between financing bank offices and field agencies was lacking. It has been observed that credit camps have not made the desired impact in boosting agricultural lendings although the overall recovery of advances is satisfactory. However, the recovery in government sponsored programmes is quite low. Political interference and willful default are the main reasons for low recovery.

Evaluation and Monitoring Cell, in the Economic Research Department of State Bank of India has conducted a study (1987)[28] on the "Impact of Bank Credit on Weaker Sections" financed under the Differential Rate of Interest Scheme. It has been observed that the utilization of bank loans have generally raised the levels of income and employment of the borrowers, who in turn have found it possible to improve their quality of life at least in quantitative terms. The number of borrowers above the poverty line in the post-loan period was almost double the number in the pre-loan period.

Banerjee and Datta (1989)[29] have noted that identification of the beneficiaries and target group is the most crucial element for fulfilling the stated objectives of the projects meant for the weaker sections. Identification of the families and specific schemes for their requirements and needs must be assessed and matched sincerely before any monetary help is provided. Provision of inputs required at the proper time is much more beneficial than provision of mere money.

Parthasarathy and Kalyani (1995)[30] studied the economic impact of women's thrift and credit societies in Cudappah district of Andhra Pradesh. The study was focussed on the economic impact of the thrift societies to study access to credit, cost of credit, savings, production and quality of life. These credit associations can serve the interest of the people as they are playing an important role in poverty alleviation in rural areas on democratic lines.

Biswajit Mondal (2007)[31] in the study of "Kisan Credit Card Scheme – A key to improve farmers accessibility – to bank credit" observed that besides the existing facilities of providing crop loan, the scope of KCC scheme has been enlarge to include term loans for agriculture and allied activities and a reasonable component to meet the consumption needs. Further, to provide adequate and timely credit support from the banking system to the farmers for their cultivation needs and to improve farmers accessibility to bank credit for production purposes, the credit delivery mechanism is being simplified and more flexibility in the use of KCC is being introduced.

Patel, A.R (2002)[32] in his study on "Rural Credit System–Need for Revamping" observed, it is strongly felt that while multi-agency approach to rural credit delivery system is a must for a country of our size and diversified socio-economic environment, there is immediate need for re-engineering the system through the implementation of well studied and conceived recommendations of earlier expert committees; improving operational efficiency of the rural credit system to make system vibrant and responding to the changing requirements taking place inside India and in the global economy and removing the regulatory rigidities.

Rakesh Malhotra (2002) [33] in the study of Regional Rural Banks – The Forgotten Case in Financial Sector Reforms analysed that if tangible reforms are not infused in RRBs to make them vibrant, these institutions may fail to achieve the very objective for which they were conceived, and decay to oblivion. As is said "A reform is correction of abuses; a revolution is transfer of power" there is a need for revolution in RRB reforms.

Badruzzama Siddiqui (2001)[34] in the study of Priority Sectors Lending – Some Major Issues observed that the policy on priority sectors lending assumed great significance after the nationalization of the major banks. The policy has come to be regarded as one of the most important ones aiming at attaining the socio-economic goals. The principle objectives of the new schemes were to achieve a wide spread of bank credit, avoiding concentration, and directing a large volume of credit flow to the hitherto neglected sectors. These sectors were given due priority not because of their tremendous potential of employment generation and various other benefits they confer on the weaker sections but also because of their significant contribution to the national income.

Identification of Research Gaps

The review of the various studies relating to the agricultural credit and Regional Rural Banks reveals that they have either focussed on macro perspective of outstanding credit or on some issues related to the specific category of the priority sector at the micro-level. None of the studies have taken an integrated view of the concept agriculture sector as priority sector credit in general and Cauvery Grameena Bank in Mysore district in particular, based on outstanding as well as incremental credit. In order to fill that gap the present study is undertaken.

References

1. Arvinder Singh Chawla (1986): Banking Developments in Patiala district, Department of Business Management, Punjab University, Patiala (Mimeo).

2. Bank of India (1975): The impact of its direct financing activities in Sholapur district, Bank of India Publication.
3. Wadhwa, C.D (1980): "Rural Banks for Rural Development", Rawat Publications, Jaipur.
4. Satya Sai (1986): Institutional Credit to Agriculture in West *Godhavari district of Andhra Pradesh*, Serials Publications, New Delhi.
5. Shylendra (1992): The economic impact of Regional Rural Banks in Karnataka (RRBs – TGB) loans, thesis submitted to University of Mysore, Mysore unpublished.
6. Rai *et al.* (1975): *The Role of Institutional Credit in Kalyanapur Block of Kanpur District, Uttar Pradesh*, Serials Publications, New Delhi.
7. Vijayakumar (1975): *Credit Requirements and Its Impact on Irrigated and Unirrigated Farms in Bangalore South Taluk*, Chethana Book House, Mysore.
8. Rao and Wahan (1974): *Agricultural Finance by Commercial Banks in South Canara District of Karnataka*, Mangala Publications, Mangalore.
9. Kavarjital *et al.* (1981): *The impact of Impact of Farm Loans on Farm Income and Employment Pattern in Panagar Block of Jabalpur district*, Deep and Deep Publications, New Delhi.
10. Hanumanthaiah (1979): *The Commercial Banks Performance in Financing Agriculture in the Parchuree Block of Prakasham district of Andhra Pradesh*, Concept Publishing House, New Delhi.
11. Kutty *et al.* (1974): The impact of Long-term — credit on Agriculture in Uthanagar Taluk of Dharmapuri district of Tamilnadu. Southern Economist, Bangalore.
12. Jugale (1997): *The Term Loan for Agricultural Purpose Granted by Zonal Development Bank*, Serials Publications, New Delhi.
13. Veerashekarappa (1997): *Institutional Finance for Rural Development*. ISEC, Bangalore.
14. Sasi Rekha, K.N and J.Rani Ratna Prabha (2008): *Agricultural Credit in India in Pre- and Post-reform Period*, Southern Economist, Vol.47, No.12, October 2008.
15. Reddy Y.V (2004): "Rural Credit: Status and Agenda", RBI Bulletin, December, pp. 1087-1089.

16. Deshpande, R.S and Nagesh Prabhu (2005): " Farmers Distress" *Economic and Political Weekly*, October 29, pp 4663-4665.
17. Chandrasekhar Rao, G (1989): "How are Rural Commercial Banks", Yojana, Vol.45, July 16-31.
18. Nand Pandey, (1989): *Commercial Banks and Rural Development*, Deep and Deep Publications, New Delhi.
19. Deshpande.V.D. (1989): *Reaching the Poor* (A Work of a Voluntary Organisation—Shranijivi Janata Sehyak Mandal, Koynanagar, District-Satara, Maharashtra); Sponsored by the Ford Foundation, and coordinated by National Institute of Bank Management, Pune (Mimeo).
20. State Bank of Patiala (1989): *Rural Lending—A Study in Patiala District*; vol. II; Head Office, The Mall, Patiala (Mimeo).
21. Singh, Pasricha. (1991): *Bank Finance and Rural Development in Punjab : A Case Study of Lead Bank Scheme*; Ph.D. Thesis; Department of Business Management; Punjabi University, Patiala.
22. Giriyappa., S. (1993): *Rural Development in Action*, Daya Publishing House, Delhi.
23. Kaladhar. (1997): *The Design, Structure and Governance of Micro-Finance in India*, Yojana, Vol.35, New Delhi.
24. Upadhaya and Kaveri. (1982): " Impact of Bank Finance on the Decentralised Sector", Commerce, Vol. 145.
25. Evaluation Survey of Utilization of Loans Advanced by Commercial Banks to Weaker Sections of Community in Punjab; the Economic Adviser to Government, Punjab, Chandigarh (1983).
26. Patel & Shete. (1984): Some Aspects of Recovery of Loans of Weaker Sections Under Priority Sector Lending, Prajanan, Vol. XIII, No.1.Jan-March.
27. A Study for Assessing the Impact Rural Lending by Commercial Banks in Patiala District of Punjab State; State Bank of Patiala; Head Office. The Mall. Patiala; 1987 (Mimeo).
28. Evaluation and Monitoring Cell; Economic Research Department of State Bank of India; "Impact of Bank Credit on Weaker Sections in Kerala" State Bank of India Monthly Review, Vol. XXVI, No. 9, Sep. 1987, pp. 444-58.

29. Banerjee and Datta. (1989): Impact of Voluntary Agency on Rural Development: A Study of Manipal Industrial Trust, Manipal. Karnataka; National Institute of Bank Management, Pune (Mimeo).

30. Parthasarathy and Kalyani, (1995): The economic impact of women's thrift and credit societies in Cudappah district of Andhra Pradesh, Kurukshetra, Vol.48, New Delhi.

31. Biswajit Mondal (2007): Kisan Credit Card Scheme — A Key to improve farmers accessibility - To bank credit, Kisan World, Vol. 34, No. 6.

32. Patel, A.R (2002): *Rural Credit System – Need for Revamping,* Kurukshetra, Vol.50, No.10.

33. Rakesh Malhotra (2002): *Regional Rural Banks – The Forgotten Case in Financial Sector Reforms,* Kurukshetra, Vol.50, No.10.

34. Badruzzama Siddiqui (2001) Priority Sector Lending - Some Major Issues, Kurukshetra, Vol. 50, No. 10.

3

Growth of Regional Rural Banks in India: An Overview

Introduction

The present chapter deals with the growth of regional rural banks in India and the institutional finance to agricultural development, the origin and objectives of the Regional Rural Bank, Branch Expansion of Rural Banks and finally the role of Regional Rural Banks in agricultural credit in India.

Agriculture plays a crucial role in the developemnt of the Indian economy. It accounts for about 19 per cent of GDP and about two-thirds of the population is dependent on the sector. The importance of farm credit as a critical input to agriculture is reinforced by the unique role of Indian agriculture in the macro-economic framework and its role in poverty alleviation. Recognising the importance of agriculture sector in India's development, the Government and the Reserve Bank of India have played a vital role in creating a broad-based institutional framework for catering to the increasing credit requirements of the sector. Agricultural policies in India have been reviewed from time-to-time to maintain pace with the changing requirements of the agriculture sector, which forms an important segment of the priority sector lending of scheduled commercial banks and target of 18 per cent of net bank credit has been stipulated for the sector. The Approach Paper to the Eleventh Five Year Plan has set a target of 4 per cent for the agriculture sector within the overall GDP growth target of 9 per cent. In this context, the need for affordable, sufficient and timely supply of institutional credit to agriculture has assumed critical importance.

The rural areas suffer from poor infrastructural facilities. The villages are yet to emerge as the main centres of production activity. The productivity is to produce goods in urban areas, even to meet the basic needs of rural consumers. This apart, the rural population requires not one but a few inputs and services. These have to be provided at the right time and in the right sequence. This demands the right kind of co-ordination amongst agencies extending help to the rural sector.[1]

It has been rightly pointed out that a purely agricultural country remains backward even in respect of agriculture. Much of the labour force in India depends on agriculture, not because it is remunerative but because there are no alternative empolyment opportunities. This is a major cause for the backwardness reportedly seen in the Indian agricultural sector. We must opt for a type of rural industrialisation which extends full support to the agricultural sector. A part of the labour force now engaged in agriculture needs to be shifted to non-agricultural occupations.

The new agricultural technology is responsible for the present comfortable foodgrain position. But the Green Revolution too has created some problems. Moreover, the first phase of the Revolution is said to have reached the saturation point. Agricultural scientists are laying stress on its second phase which alone can give the real boost needed for India's agricultural sector. Irrigation has emerged as a crucial input contributing to the success of the Revolution. The farmers no doubt require price incentives, but their problems can be solved only when there is a steady increase in agricultural productivity. Technology should be cost-effective and give good financial returns to the farming community.[2]

Given the unfavourable power structure in rural India, the benefits of the revolution even the anti-poverty programmes do not reach to benefit the rural population. The workers and small producers in India cannot put in their best in an inequitous atmosphere. Therefore, production suffers. Also, the rural sector cannot take advantage of opportunities available so long as the institutions and dominated by the rich.

Agricultural Credit in India in Pre- and Post-reform Period

Indian agriculture is shifted with the fertile land and abundant availability of water resources. It had a long history of the fertile plains of Northern India irrigated by the Indus, the Ganga-Jamuna river systems and the Brahmaputra in the East. Southern India has its own river systems. So the prosperity of India is based mainly on the development of agriculture because majority of its populaiton is engaged directly or indirectly in agriculture. Hence, the development of agriculture would mean the development of the rural masses and developemnt of India. Further, increase in agriculutral productivity depends on the adoption of new farm practices such as high yielding variety seeds, chemical fertilisers, pesticides, insecticides, farm machinery and assured irrigation facilities.[3]

The adoption of these practices depends on the availability of larger and larger amounts of finance. The creation of adequate and requisite credit avenues is therefore essential for agricultural progress. Credit is a condition that enables a farmer to extend his controlover his ownership of resources. It represents mobilization of the savings by financial intermediaries or government from the people and through such credit operations financial savings are transformed into capital, the money obtained through credit provides a command enough funds to explore opportunities. Most of the developing countries, aiming to strengthen their agriculture have evolved rural financial institutions to provide agricultural credit. Credit plays the role of an accelerator for agricultural development.[4]

Agricultural credit refers to credit provided to the rural population. It covers loans to agriculture as well as loans to non-agriculturists, artisans and landless labourers who are residing in rural areas. The objective of agricultural credit is to provide adequate finance for agriculture, animal husbandry, rural industry, rural trade, rural transport and all other economic activities of the countryside. The necessity of credit in India arose because majority of farmers and non-agricultural population suffer from financial anemia at present and that the injection of sufficient quantities of finance into them could accelerate their pace and increases the value and volume of their production. The ideal agricultural credit scheme should aim at providing and ensuring adequate finance to every person in the countryside, who is engaged in or willing to engage in any economic activity.[5]

The importance of agricultural credit in a country like India, which is essentially rural in nature hardly, needs elaboration, economic development of the countryside hinges upon availability of credit to rural economy. The burden of indebtedness in rural India is great, and falls mainly on the households of rural working people. The exploitation of this group in the credit market is one of the most pervasive and persistent features of rural life in India. Despite major structural changes in credit institutions and forms of agricultural credit in the post-independence period, Darwin's statement (1925)[6] that "the Indian peasant is born in debt, lives in debt and bequeaths debt", still remains true for the great majority of agricultural households in the countryside. Rural households need credit for a variety of reasons.

The rural economic activity is highly seasonal in nature and households need credit to smooth out seasonal fluctuations in earnings and expenditure. Credit is necessary both for meeting the short-term requirements for working capital and for long-term investment in agriculture and other income-bearing activities. Rural households, particularly those vulnerable to what appear to others to be minor shocks with respect to income and expenditure, need credit as an insurance against risk. Realization of the gravity of the problem of agricultural credit by the government at different levels and at different periods is well reflected in appointment of several committees and commissions to examine the problem of agricultural credit before and after independence.[7]

Agricultural credit is disbursed with the help of a multi-agency network consisting of Commercial Banks (CBs), Regional Rural Banks (RRBs) and Cooperatives. Approximately there are 100,000 village-level Primary Agricultural Credit Societies (PACS), 368 District Central Cooperative Banks (DCCBs) with 12,858 branches and 30 State Cooperative Banks (SCBs) with 953 branches. These are providing primarily short and medium-term agricultural credit. Long-term cooperative structure consists of 19 State Cooperative Agricultural and Rural Development Banks (SCARDBs), with 2609 operational units as on 31 March, 2005 comprising 788 branches and 772 Primary Agricultural and Rural Development Banks (PA & RDBs) with 1049 branches. The credit needs of the farmers can be seen from two angles; *(i)* on the basis of time and (ii)on the basis of purpose.[8]

Evolution and Structure of Institutional Finance

Institutional finance for agriculture in India dates back to 1793 when the system of taccavi loans initiated. Agriculture finance is given priority by the government for the rural credit system. Earlier the finance was provided to the farmers departmentally and grants as well as cooperative system. In the pre-independence period, agricultural credit to farmers was exclusively provided by cooperative banking system (1904). Such credit has no explicit relationship with input supply or farm investment and seen as an alternative to the village money-lender. The State Cooperative Agriculture and Rural Development Banks (SCARDB) then called the land mortgage banks provided long-term loans to repay the old debts.[9]

The evolution of institutional credit to agriculture could be broadly classified into four distinct phases – 1904 – 1969 (predominance of cooperatives and setting up of RBI), 1969-1975(nationalization of commercial banks and setting up of Regional Rural Banks), 1975-1990 (setting up of NABARD) and from 1991 onwards (financial sector reforms). The genesis of institutional involvement in the sphere of agricultural credit could be traced back to the enactment of the cooperative Societies Act in 1904. The establishment of the RBI in 1935 reinforced the process of institutional development for agricultural credit. The RBI is perhaps the first central bank in the world to have taken interest in the matters related to agriculture and agricultural credit, and it continues to do so.

A historic step in the rural banking system has happened with the nationalization of 14 commercial banks (1969). Banking moved from class banking to mass banking and also led to the opening of new branches to unbanked areas and increase in rural lending.[10] With the introduction of production oriented system and Green Revolution cooperatives alone would not be able to meet the credit needs of farmers. Regional Rural Banks (1975) were set up exclusively for the small, marginal farmers, agricultural labourers, artisans and small entrepreneurs for development of agriculture, trade, commerce, and other productive activities. RRBs are state sponsored and work in partnership with commercial banks. They were mainly controlled by rural based staffs that were expected to be better suited to the needs of rural population.

Rural credit is available from the different sources. The credit system in rural India can be classified as; institutional credit (formal banking system); it includes Cooperatives, Commercial Banks and Regional Rural Banks and non-institutional credit sources (informal sources). It includes professional money-lenders, agriculture money-lenders, commission agents, merchants, friends, relatives and others.

The National Bank for Agriculture and Rural Development is an apex development bank of the country for promoting sustainable and equitable agriculture and rural development through effective credit support, related services, building institutions, and other innovative initiatives. NABARD today is at the center of the development activities in the rural areas and bedrock of prosperous rural India.

The most important development in the field of agricultural credit is the setting up of the National Bank for Agriculture and Rural Development in July 1982. NABARD is an apex organisation in respect of all matters relating to policy, planning and operational aspects, concerning the flow of credit for development of agriculture, rural industries and handicrafts and other allied activities in the rural areas. It is a single integrated agency for meeting the credit needs of all types of agricultural and rural development. It has taken over the entire operations of the Agricultural Refinance and Development Corporation (ARDC) as well as refinance functions of RBI.

NABARD has been guiding all major agencies operating in the rural credit market, namely the Commercial Banks, the Regional Rural Banks and the cooperative credit institutions. NABARD has been envisaged as the leader of the entire rural credit system. The main functions of NABARD are as follows;

1. NABARD works as an apex body for development policy, planning, operational matters, coordination, monitoring, research, training and consultancy etc., relating to rural credit.
2. It provides refinance to the cooperatives, regional rural banks and commercial banks for short, medium and long-term requirements.
3. It undertakes the inspection of cooperative banks and regional rural banks and advises the government on related matters.

NABARD has thus been playing a pivotal role in channelisation of bank credit to the rural sector. It provides refinance and improves the resource base of institutions providing credit to the rural sector. In recent years NABARD has attempted to enhance the coverage of rural credit institutions by bringing in areas of non-traditional agriculture and new ventures in farm activities under their preview. NABARD is also taking steps to restructure the institutional credit system.[11]

The institutional credit system in rural India has following agencies known as rural financial institutions catering to the banking needs of the rural masses:

(a) Short-term cooperative credit structure (SCB, DCCB and PACS).

(b) Long-term cooperative credit structure (LDB/ARDB)

(c) Commercial Banks.

(d) Regional Rural Banks.

Flow of Agricultural Credit

To improve credit flow to the agriculture sector, the Government initiated a number of policy measures, from time to time, like farm credit package and Special Agricultural Credit Plans (SACP). The Union Finance Minister in his budget speech for 2006-07 had urged the banks (including cooperative banks and RRBs) to disburse Rs.1,75,000 crore as credit to agriculture sector during 2006-07. The overall achievement during 2006-07 was Rs. 2,03,296 crore. Also, new farmers covered under the institutional credit system were 8.35 million as against the target of 5 million. Encouraged by the achievement, Budget 2007-08 set a higher target of Rs. 2,25,000 crore for disbursement of credit and further addition of 5 million new farmers as borrowers to the banking system. Up to 2007- 08, the flow of credit to this sector was Rs.1,37,760 crore which is about 61 per cent of the target (Table 3.1).

Table 3.1

Institutional Credit to Agriculture and Allied Activities (Rs. Crore)

Agencies	*2002-03*	*2003-04*	*2004-05*	*2005-06*	*2006-07*	*2007-08*
Cooperative Banks	23,716.38	26,958.79	31,424.23	39,403.77	42,479.80	33,070.17
RRBs	6,069.79	7,581.15	12,404.00	15,222.90	20,434.65	15,924.56
Commercial Banks	39,773.60	52,440.85	81,481.14	1,25,858.90	1,40,381.93	88,764.83
Total	**69,559.77**	**86,980.79**	**1,25,309.37**	**1,80,485.57**	**2,03,296.38**	**1,37,759.56**

Source: NABARD Report, 2007-08.

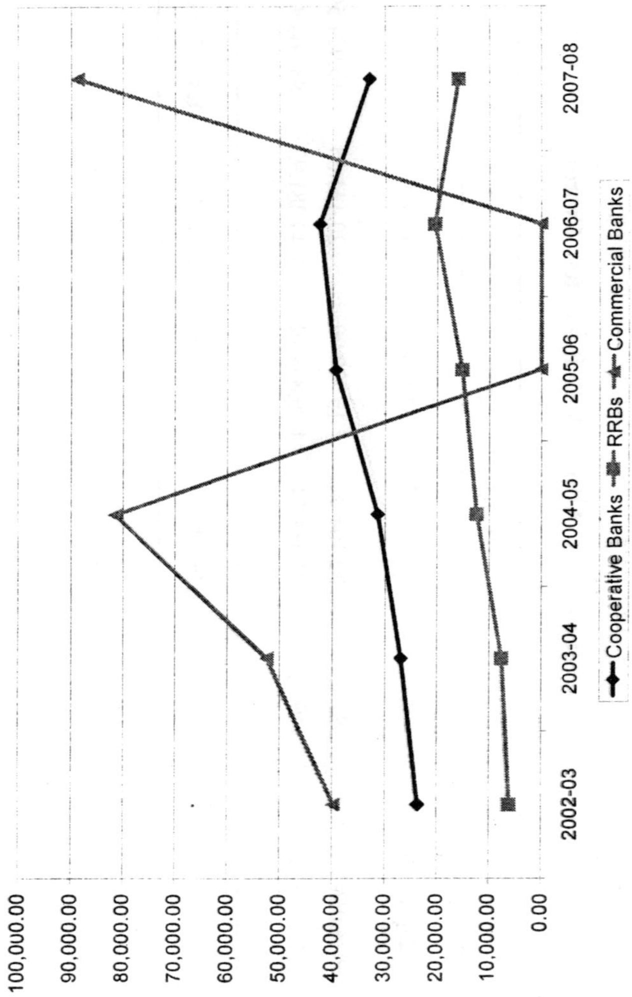

Kisan Credit Card (KCC) Scheme

To provide adequate and timely credit support to the farmers from the formal banking system in a flexible, hassle-free and cost-effective manner the Kisan Credit Card scheme was introduced in 1998-99. The KCC scheme has now been extended to borrowers of the long-term cooperative credit structure, thus paving the way for acceptance of KCC scheme as a single window for a comprehensive credit product.

Features of Kisan Credit Card

Farmers with rainfall crops, tenant farmers are eligible for the KCC card. Even illiterate farmers can also have Kisan credit card. Credit limit is based on the cropping pattern and landholding using latest scales of finance. It provides for any number of drawls/repayments at the convenience of the farmers. Each drawl is to be repaid within a maximum period of 12 months. The Card is valid for 3 years so that there is no need for execution of loan documents every year. Further, credit balance in Kisan Credit Card account may earn interest like in a savings bank account.

Benefits of Kisan Credit Card Scheme

As against the old system which was evidently restrictive the scheme has several advantages over the traditional mode of providing access to short-term credit. Firstly, the cards as envisaged under the scheme can be used like ordinary credit cards and have provisions such as revolving cash credit facility involving any number of withdrawals and repayments within the prescribed limit. Secondly, the limit on credit is fixed on the basis of operational landholding, cropping pattern and scale of production credit requirement. Thirdly, there is flexibility for repayment of loan and repayment is made through techniques accompanied by card-cum-passbook. Fourth, in case of crop failure of damage to the crops due to natural calamities, the system allows borrowers to get their loans rescheduled. Fifth, the card is valid for three years and is subject to only an annual review, which means fewer formalities in completing the paperwork sixth a new feature that has been introduced recently provides for a personal insurance cover ranging from Rs. 25,000 to all cardholders, against permanent disability or accidental death.

From, 2000-01 onwards the cardholders are begin provided personal accident insurance, which covers risks against death, permanent disability due to accident caused by external, violent or other visible means with a maximum sum assured for Rs. 50,000. The premium for insurance is shared between banks and cardholders in the ratio of 2:1 and the rate of premium is Rs.15 for one year and Rs. 45 for three years respectively. The claim settlement procedure is supposed to be simple and requires enquire cum verification committee, branch manager of the implementing bank. Lead bank officer and a representative of the insurance company to certify the nature of accident that caused disability/death and recommend settlement of insurance claims.

The crop loans for eligible crops cultivated by Kisan holders are insured under Rastriya Krishi Bima Yojana (RKBY) for this the banks are required to maintain all records, cut-off dates for submitting declarations and end use. The sum insured covers the value of threshold vied of crops covered under RKBY with an option to cover up to 150 per cent of the average yield for crops on payment of extra premium. There is a 50 per cent subsidy on the premium paid by marginal and small farmers, which is shared equally by the Central Government and the State Government.

Further KCC provides flexibility to the farmer to draw cash from a branch other than issuing branch and to buy inputs from any supplier of his choice. Due to frequent drawal and payment of loans, it provides reduction in Quentin of interest to the farmer. There is also an improvement in the recovery of loans because of frequent banker borrower contacts.

Studies reveal that major change witnessed after farmers received KCCs is that there has been a significant drop in the number of borrowers borrowing exdusively from informal sources to meet their short-term credit needs. At the same time there is a considerable increase in the number of borrowers who borrow from both formal and informal sources and to a certain extent excessively from formal sources as well. Along with these changes another significant development that has occurred in rural financial markets is that the cost of borrowing from informal sources, mainly money lenders has also exhibited marginal decrease after the introduction of KCCs.

To give further fillip to the KCC scheme, NABARD advised all RRBs to achieve the targets of issuing at least 150 KCCs be each branch of RRB during 2007-08. Since inception of the KCC scheme, the banking system has issued 707.55 lakh KCCs up to November 30, 2007 (Table 3.2).

Table 3.2

Agency-wise KCCs Issued

(Rs.lakh)

Year	*Cooperative Banks*	*RRBs*	*Commercial Banks*	*Total*
1998-99	1.56	0.06	6.22	7.84
1999-00	35.95	1.73	13.66	51.34
2000-01	56.14	6.48	23.90	86.52
2001-02	54.36	8.34	30.71	93.41
2002-03	45.79	9.64	27.00	82.43
2003-04	48.78	12.75	30.94	92.47
2004-05	35.56	17.29	43.95	96.80
2005-06	25.98	12.49	41.65	80.12
2006-07	22.97	14.06	48.08	85.11
2007-08	14.01	10.29	7.21	31.51
Total	341.10	93.13	273.32	707.55
% share	**48.21**	**13.16**	**38.63**	**100.00**

Source: NABARD and RBI, 2007-08.

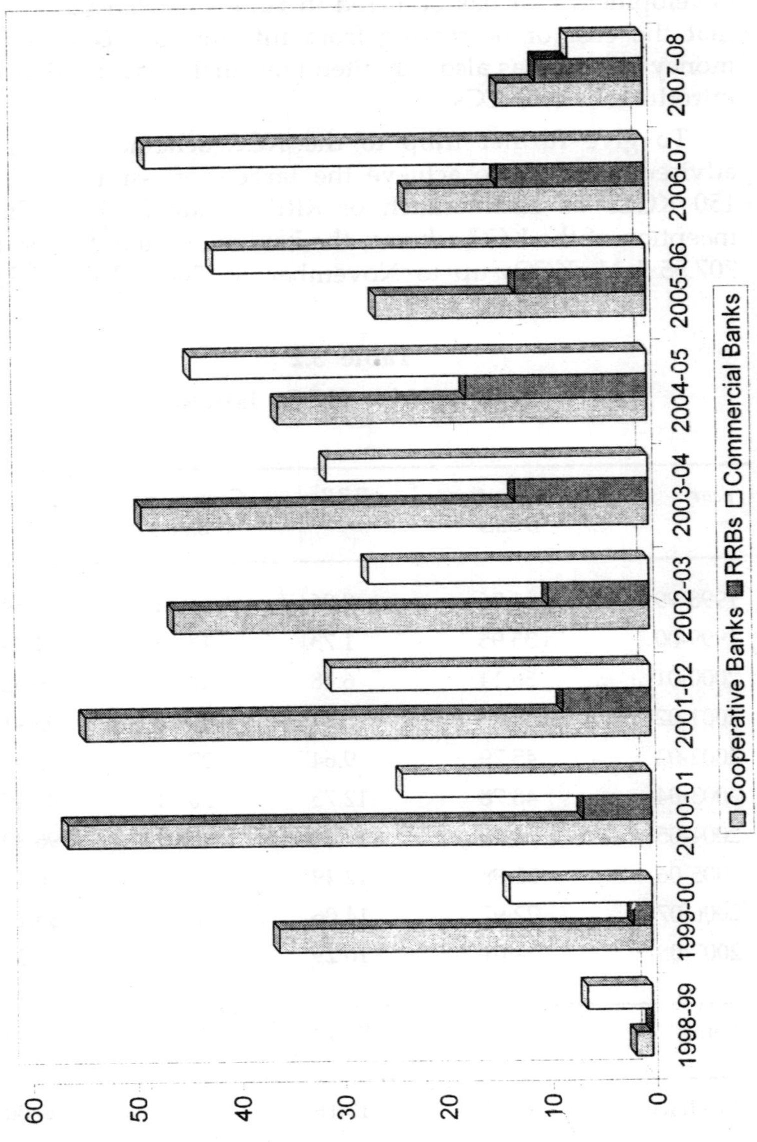
60
50
40
30
20
10
0
1998-99
1999-00
2000-01
2001-02
2002-03
2003-04
2004-05
2005-06
2006-07
2007-08
Cooperative Banks
RRBs
Commercial Banks

During 2006-07, the total number of KCCs issued were 85.11 lakh and the amount scantiness was Rs. 46,729 crore. As per the available information for 2007-08 the amount sanctioned was Rs. 25,263 crore.

With the renewed emphasis by the government on increasing credit flow to the agriculture sector, NABARD advised cooperative banks and RRBs to identify and cover all farmers including defaulters, oral lessees, tenant farmers, sharecroppers and others, who might have been left outside the fold of the KCC scheme for any reason, as also new farmers so that all farmers are covered under the scheme by March 31, 2007. Further, the banks were advised to issue KCCs in a hassle-free manner and extend crop loans only through KCC and renew them so as to ensure quality in operations. To make the operation more user-friendly and comprehensive in its coverage of credit needs of the farmers through a single window, NABARD has extended the scope of KCC to cover term loans for agriculture and allied activities and reasonable component for consumption loan. The scheme has also been extended to the clientele of the State Cooperative Agriculture and Rural Development Banks.

Agency-wise, cooperative banks account for about 62 per cent share of total number of cards issued upto January 2004. Of the remaining 38 per cent share, commercial banks account for around 28 per cent and the share of RRBs was only 10 per cent. In terms of total advances sanctioned to cardholders, the share of cooperative banks was 59 per cent followed by 30.5 per cent for commercial banks and 10.5 per cent for RRBs.

State-Wise Progress of KCC

The following Table 3.3 provides the information on the number of KCC issued and amount sanction under this scheme across states in India.

It is revealed that among the various states of the country, the maximum number of KCCs have been issued in Uttar

Pradesh (74.3 lakh) followed by Andhra Pradesh (60.7 lakh) and Maharastra (37.2 lakh) in that order, respectively.

In terms of the cumulative amount sanctioned through KCCs, however, there is a slight alteration in the rankings of these states. Maharashtra edges out Uttar Pradesh marginally and emerges at the top in terms of amount sanctioned through KCCs. Thus two other major states Uttar Pradesh and Andhra Pradesh, which rank first and second in terms of total number of KCCs issued occupy second and third place in terms of amount sanctioned through KCCs.

Table 3.3

Number of KCCs Issued and Amount Sanctioned (upto January ,2007-08)

Sl. No.	*State*	*Number of KCCs*		*Amount Sanctioned*	
		Number	*% of total for all India*	*Amount (Rs Crore)*	*% of total for all India*
1.	*2.*	*3.*	*4.*	*5.*	*6.*
1.	Andhra Pradesh	60,66,000	16.4	971	11.2
2.	Assam	75,000	0.2	8	0.1
3.	Bihar	13,47,000	3.7	175	2.0
4.	Gujarat	16,00,000	4.3	582	6.7
5.	Goa	5,000	0.0	6	0.1
6.	Haryana	14,07,000	3.8	628	7.2
7.	Himachal Pradesh	1,03,000	0.3	23	0.3
8.	J & K	37,000	0.1	6	0.1
9.	Karnataka	23,09,000	6.3	724	8.3
10.	Kerala	12,93,000	3.5	252	2.9
11.	Madhya Pradesh	23,05,000	6.2	701	8.1

1.	2.	3.	4.	5.	6.
12.	Maharastra	37,17,000	10.1	1199	13.8
13.	Orissa	21,56,000	5.8	302	3.5
14.	Punjab	13,37,000	3.6	659	7.6
15.	Rajasthan	22,44,000	6.1	686	7.9
16.	Tamil Nadu	24,83,000	6.7	482	5.5
17.	Uttar Pradesh	74,31,000	20.1	1165	134
18.	West Bengal	9,14,000	2.5	118	1.4
19.	Other N.E states	31,000	0.1	4	0.0
20.	Union Territories	22,000	0.1	5	0.1
All India		**3,68,82,000**	**100.00**	**8696**	**100.00**

Source: NABARD, Bangalore, 2007-08.

From the above Table 3.3, it can be observed that barring the exceptions of Assam, Himachal Pradesh, Kerala, and Union Territories, the maximum share of KCC is cornered by the Cooperative Banks.

As far as the amount sanctioned through KCC is concerned in Assam, Goa, Himachal Pradesh, Karnataka, Kerala, Uttar Pradesh and Union Territories, the maximumshare of amount sanctioned through KCCs is accounted for by the Commercial banks. In all other states cooperative banks dominate the scene. Similarly in Jammu and Kashmir, the amount sanctioned by RRBs is close to the amount sanctioned by the Cooperative Banks. In Bihar and Tamil Nadu also the amount sanctioned by Commercial Banks noteworthy.

The Table 3.5 examines shares of different states and region of the country in total number of operational holdings as per 1995-96 census and number of KCCs issued as a ratio of number holdings. The resulting estimates clearly indicates quite mismatch in the number of holdings and progress made in issuing KCCs particularly in case of states like Bihar, Orissa,

Table 3.4
Shares of Cooperative Banks, RRBs and Commercial Banks in Total KCCs Issued and Amount Sanctioned (State-wise) up to January, 2007-08)

(Percentage)

Sl. No	State	Cooperative Banks		Regional Rural Banks		Commercial Banks	
		Number	Amount	Number	Amount	Number	Amount
1.	Andhra Pradesh	56.6	55.4	112.7	12.4	30.7	32.2
2.	Assam	1.9	1.7	28.0	35.1	70.1	63.2
3.	Bihar	68.1	51.2	6.0	7.2	32.2	41.6
4.	Gujarat	59.8	68.4	7.4	7.0	32.8	24.5
5.	Goa	55.3	10.2	0.0	0.0	44.7	89.8
6.	Haryana	75.3	71.0	5.9	8.5	18.8	20.5
7.	Himachal Pradesh	28.9	22.9	3.7	40.0	9.1	11.3
8.	J & K	79.3	48.7	11.7	40.0	9.1	11.3
9.	Karnataka	44.4	32.3	18.6	23.8	37.0	43.9
10.	Kerala	38.0	35.1	15.8	19.5	46.2	45.4
11.	Madhya Pradesh	73.6	73.5	7.3	5.5	19.1	21.0
12.	Maharashtra	78.6	80.3	2.5	2.8	18.9	16.9
13.	Orissa	81.0	82.8	6.7	7.7	12.3	9.5
14.	Punjab	56.2	52.5	3.1	5.7	40.7	41.8
15.	Rajasthan	79.4	70.0	4.9	9.5	15.7	20.5
16.	Tamil Nadu	51.5	55.8	4.0	1.5	44.4	42.7
17.	Uttar Pradesh	57.7	36.6	16.6	21.1	25.8	42.3
18.	West Bengal	56.7	56.0	8.2	8.0	35.1	36.0
19.	Other N.E states	21.7	20.4	26.0	30.4	52.3	49.3
20.	Union Territories	30.1	25.0	0.0	0.0	69.9	75.0
	All India	62.0	58.9	10.0	10.6	28.0	30.6

Punjab, West Bengal, Madhya Pradesh, Gujarat and Haryana. The ratios of number of KCCs issued to number of land-holdings indicated that among major states of the country, progress in Punjab and Haryana is remarkable where the ratios work out to be 122.3 per cent and 81.4 per cent respectively. The ratio exceeding 100 in the case of Punjab indicates that for some operational holdings, there is more than one KCC. The progress in Orissa and Andhra Pradesh is also significant given the tact in that about 50 per cent of landholdings seem to have been covered. In some other states such as Tamil Nadu, Uttar Pradesh, Maharashtra, Karnataka, Rajasthan and Gujarat these ratios are the range of 31 to 42 per cent.

Table 3.5
Number of Operational Landholdings vis-a-vis Number of KCCs issued (up to January, 2007-08)

Sl. No	*State*	*No of Holdings*	*Number of KCCs as a ratio of Number of land holdings*
1.	2.	3.	4.
1.	Andhra Pradesh	1,06,03,000 (9.2%)	57.2
2.	Assam	26,83,000 (2.3%)	2.8
3.	Bihar	1,41,55,000 (12.2%)	9.5
4.	Gujarat	37,81,000 (3.3%)	42.3
5.	Goa	70,000 (0.1%)	7.1
6.	Haryana	17,28,000 (1.5%)	81.4
7.	Himachal Pradesh	8,63,000 (0.7%)	11.9
8.	J & K	13,36,000 (1.2%)	2.8
9.	Karnataka	62,21,000 (5.4%)	37.1
10.	Kerala	62,99,000 (5.4%)	20.5
11.	Madhya Pradesh	96,03,000 (8.3%)	24.0

1.	2.	3.	4.
12.	Maharashtra	1,06,53,000 (9.2%)	34.9
13.	Orissa	39,66,000 (3.4%)	54.4
14.	Punjab	10,93,000 (0.9%)	122.3
15.	Rajasthan	53,64,000 (4.6%)	41.8
16.	Tamil Nadu	80,12,000 (6.9)	31.0
17.	Uttar Pradesh	2,15,29,000 (18.6%)	34.5
18.	West Bengal	65,47,000 (5.7%)	14.0
19.	Other N.E states	967,000 (0.8%)	3.2
20.	Union Territories	107,000 (0.1%)	20.6
	All India	**11,55,80,000(100%)**	**31.9**

Source : Compiled from, Sharma, Anil (2008); "The Kisan Credit Card Scheme Impact, Weaknesses and Further Reforms", NCAER, New Delhi, p. 18.

But in the remaining states the progress seems to be very slow. This is particularly true for Kerala, West Bengal, Himachal Pradesh, Bihar, Goa, Jammu & Kashmir and almost all states of the north eastern region. It has been pointed out by NABARD that progress in issuing KCCs has been encouraging in those states where state governments took active interest in following up with the financial institutions.

The Table 3.6 shows that the ratio of amount sanctioned through KCCs to total short-term credit which is being advanced every year. It is an evidence of the phenomenal growth that has occurred in the issuance of credit cards.

It is evident from the above table that by the end of 2006-07, out of the total short-term credit issued by Cooperative Banks, 80.4 per cent was through Kisan Credit Card. In the case of RRBs, the share of credit sanctioned through KCCs was a little over 60 per cent of total short-term credit disbursements during the same year. In the case of commercial banks, however, the progress was slow in comparison to

Table 3.6

Amount Sanctioned Through KCCs as Ratio of Short-Term Credit

Year	*Cooperative Banks*		*Regional Banks*		*Commercial Banks*		*Total*	
	Short-term credit (Rs. Crore)	*Amount sanctioned through KCC as a ratio of short-term credit*	*Short-term credit (Rs. Crore)*	*Amount sanctioned through KCC as a ratio of short-term credit*	*Short-term credit (Rs. Crore)*	*Amount sanctioned through KCC as a ratio of short-term credit*	*Short-term credit (Rs. Crore)*	*Amount sanctioned through KCC as a ratio of short-term credit*
1998-99	12571	6.6%	1710	0.6	9622	13.0%	23903	8.7
1999-00	14845	24.3%	2423	16.7	11697	30.2%	28965	26.1
2004-05	16583	56.8%	3245	43.2	13486	41.6%	33314	49.3
2006-07	18829	84.7%	3777	63.1	17904	42.0%	40510	63.8
2007-08	19707	80.4%	4775	61.9	21104	35.0%	45586	57.4

Source : Sharma, Anil : The Kisan Credit Card Scheme : Impact, Weakness and Further Reforms, NCAER, New Delhi, p. 14.

cooperative banks and RRBs as the amount sanctioned through KCCs constituted only 35 to 42 per cent of their total short-term advances.

In general, the share of credit sanctioned through KCCs by all three types of financial institutions works out to be approximately 60 per cent of the amount that farmers borrow for their short-term requirements.

For various reasons, particularly for lack of political will, land reforms have been neglected. The rural population requires support in terms of assets like land to improve their income levels and social status. Diversification of agriculture is needed to improve the plight of the agricultural labourers. The rural artisans and other sections would benefit only when the rural economy is diversified with stress on non-farming activities. Of course, organisation of the rural sector is needed to put an end to all kinds of exploitation continuing in the sector for a long time. And to solve this in rural areas regional rural banks play a very significant role in rural areas.

In spite of the impressive strides made by the formal channel in rural areas, Government of India had been seized with the anomaly that most of the small and marginal farmers, rural artisans, and agricultural labourers are deprived of the crucial input of timely and adequate credit from the institutional sources. The government has been taking elaborate and extensive initiatives to augment the outreach of formal channel to rural masses. One of the major initiatives taken was establishment of Regional Rural Banks in 1975.

RRBs were conceived with the notion of augmenting the outreach of the institutional channel of credit Regional Rural Banks Act, 1976; which was deemed to have come into effect with retrospective date of 26 September, 1975. Five RRBs were established in the first phase in 1975. Today, the country has 196 RRBs, employing about 70,200 persons, sponsored by 28 sponsoring banks operating in 484 districts with more than 14,300 branches.

Regional Rural Banks are state sponsored regionally based

and rural oriented commercial banks envisaged to combine simultaneously the desirable qualities of both cooperative banks and commercial banks RRB's being an important segment of the Rural financial institution in the country have carried out a special place for themselves in terms of geographical coverage clientele outreachbusiness volume and contributions for development of rural economy. RRB's are focussing their attention on the attainment of sustainable viability improved customer services, new and innovative loan products and diversified business portfolio RRB's are at par with the scheduled commercial banks in respect of priority sector lending investment and credit discipline and transparency.

Although the cooperative and commercial banks had an impressive record in terms of geographical courage and disbursement of credit. It was observed that the vast majority of the poor were generally deprived of credit and other banking facilities. In order to provide access to low-cost banking facilities to the poor, a new set-up of banks is RRBs was established in the country to meet exclusively the needs of the weaker sections of the rural population as institutions which combine the local feel and the familiarity with rural problems which the cooperative possess and the degree of business organisation ability to mobilize deposit access to central money markets and modernized outlook which the commercial banks have.[12]

The Government of India in July 1975 appointed a working group to study in depth the problem of devising alternative agencies to provide institutional credit to the rural people in the context of steps then initiated under the 20-point economic programme. The working group identified various weaknesses of the cooperative credit agencies and the commercial banks and felt that these institutions would not be able to fill the regional and functional gaps in the rural credit system within a reasonable period of time.

The Government of India promulgated the Regional Rural Banks ordinance on 26th September, 1975 which was later replaced by the Regional Rural Bank Act, 1976. The Preamble to the Act 1976 the preamble to the act states the objectives to develop rural economy by proceeding credit and facility for the development of agriculture trade commerce industry and other productive activities in the rural areas. Particularly to small marginal farmers agricultural labour artisans and small entrepreneurs. The RRBs Act empowers the Central Government to open the banks from time-to-time at places where it may consider it necessary. The Government of India jointly owns a Regional Rural Bank. The Government of concerned state and public sector bank which sponsored it. The authorized capital of each bank is Rs. 1 crore (Subsequently raised Rs. 5 crore) with paid-up capital Rs.25 Lakhs (Subsequently increased to Rs.1 crore) that is held by them in the proportion of 50, 15 and 35 per cent respectively. Each bank carries the banking business within the local limits specified by the notification.

On 26 September, 1975 a New Landmark was made in the history of Indian Banking as Regional Rural Bank ordinance was promulgated by the President of India. On 2 October 1975 as mark of tribute to father of nation five Regional Rural banks were set in four states.

1. Haryana Kshetriya Grameena Bank – Haryana
2. Jaipur–Nagpur Anchalik Grameena Bank – Jaipur
3. Prathma Grameena Bank Uttar Pradesh – Gorakpur
4. Gorakpur Kshetriya Grameena Bank – U.P.
5. Gaur Grameena Bank - West Bengal

Since then there has been enormous growth in development of RRBs, both in terms of number and branches. By end of March 1995, there were 195 RRBs covering 425 districts.

Objectives of the Regional Rural Banks in India

The preamble of the RRB Act India, "with a view to

developing the rural economy by providing for the purpose of development of agriculture, trade, commerce, industry and other productive activities in the rural areas credit and other facilities, particularly to the small and marginal farmers, agricultural labourers, artisans and small entrepreneurs and for matters connected therewith and incidental thereto."

The main objectives of setting up the RRB's is to help or assist the potential rural development of agriculture and economy of the area through providing credit and other facilities to the needful people of the rural area well in time and on reasonable terms. So that they may start some viable production activities.

The Main objectives of setting up of RRBs are given below:

1. To provide larger volume of institutional credit to agricultural sector for rapid development and thereby helping in reduction of regional imbalances in the availability of credit in rural areas.
2. To provide credit and other facilities especially to the small/marginal farmers, agricultural labourers in rural areas.
3. To supplement various credits institutions working in the field of agriculture to achieve adequate credit planning.
4. To remove the curse of poverty in rural areas.
5. To ensure continuous recycling of funds and to fill up the rural credit gap.
6. To provide employment to rural educated youth who are properly oriented to look after the needs of the rural community. These banks will provide job opportunities also by financing subsidiary occupations reviewing rural vocations and life especially rural artisans and small entrepreneurs in rural areas.
7. To improve standard of living the RRB's were considered to be a suitable institution to provide

needed credit at their doorstep on reasonable terms and conditions so that the weaker sections of people in rural areas could raise their total productivity and through it their standard of living.

8. The objectives of rural banking policy are mainly to convey an institutional arrangement to mobilise the savings of the people in rural areas.

Branch Expansion

The RRBs have made a rapid and impressive progress in terms of their number from 196, in 1999 with it same to 196 RRB's by March 2008. The data relating to geographical coverage of RRB's and their branches is shown in the Table 3.7, which denotes the growth of RRB's from 1999-2000 to 2007-08.

Table 3.7
Growth of RRBs and their Branches in India 1999-2000 to 2007-08

Year	*No. of RRBs*	*Total Branches*	*No. of Districts Covered*
1999-00	196	14475	448
2000-01	196	14499	484
2001-02	196	14524	492
2002-03	196	14313	497
2003-04	196	14390	504
2004-05	196	14433	509
2005-06	196	14485	509
2006-07	196	14490	509
2007-08	196	14500	510

Source: National Bank for Agriculture and Rural Development (NABARD) Statistics on Regional Rural Banks, 2008.

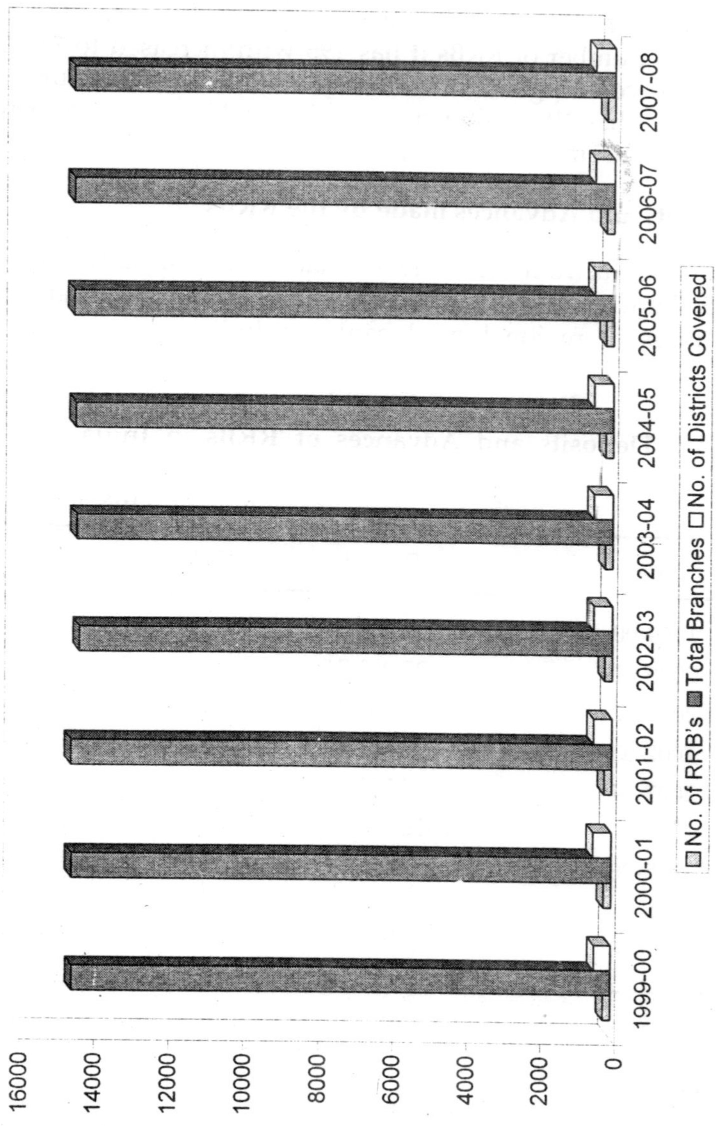
16000
14000
12000
10000
8000
6000
4000
2000
0
1999-00
2000-01
2001-02
2002-03
2003-04
2004-05
2005-06
2006-07
2007-08
No. of RRB's
Total Branches
No. of Districts Covered

During 1999-00 the total number of RRBs increased to 196 with 14,475 branches covering 448 districts. In 2001-02 the total number of RRBs it has 196 with increased to 14,524 branches covering 492 districts. By 2007-08 the total number of RRBs it has 196 with increased to 14,500 branches covering 510 districts in the country.

Deposits and Advances made by the RRBs

It is clear from the Table 3.8 that in India since December 1975, there has been a rapid growth in deposit and outstanding advances of regional rural banks in India.

Table 3.8
Deposits and Advances of RRBs in India

(Rs. in crores)

Year	*Deposits*	*Outstanding Advances*
1999-00	22,189.23	9860.51
2000-01	27,065.74	11355.84
2001-02	32,204.34	13181.57
2002-03	38,271.87	15816.30
2003-04	44,539.15	18629.22
2004-05	50,098.34	22157.84
2005-06	53,076.57	23543.09
2006-07	60,234.56	25432.49
2007-08	63,456.79	27980.98

Source: Annual Reports of NABARD on RRBs, 2007-08.

During 1999-00 the deposits of RRB's in India were Rs. 22,189.23 crore, whereas outstanding advances was Rs. 9860.61 crore. After 1999, there has been an increasing trend in both deposits and outstanding advances of RRBs in India. Deposits

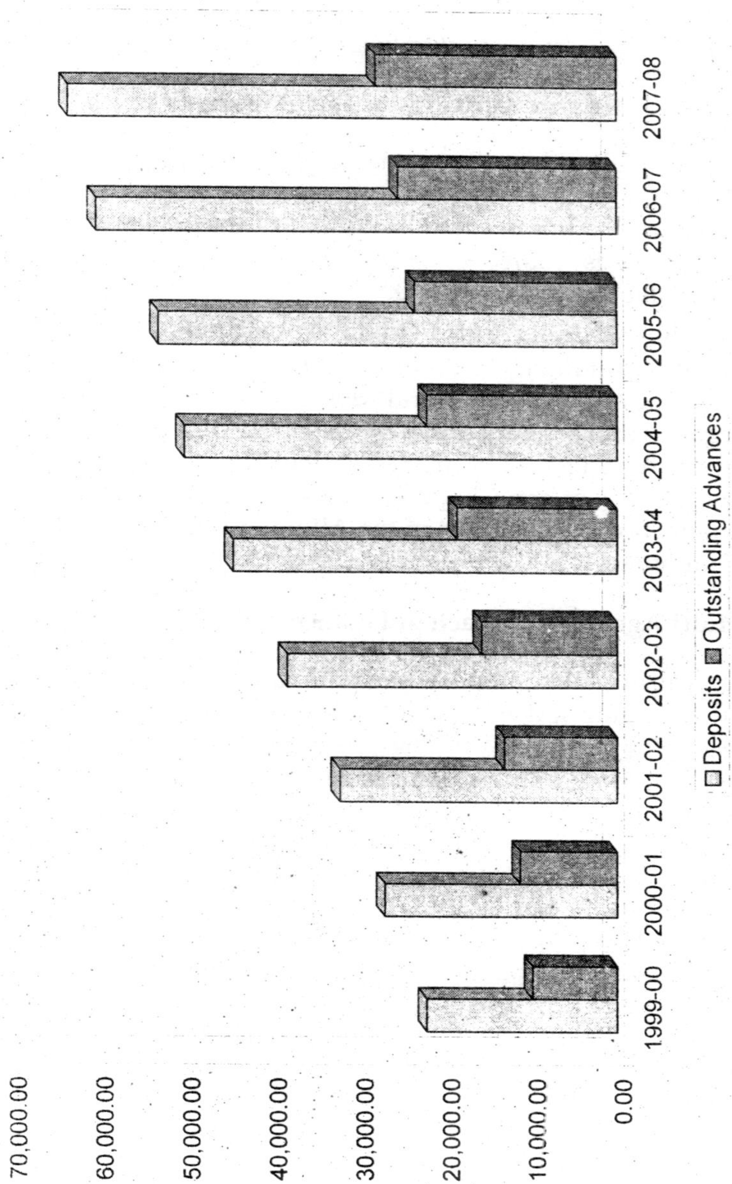
70,000.00
60,000.00
50,000.00
40,000.00
30,000.00
20,000.00
10,000.00
0.00
1999-00
2000-01
2001-02
2002-03
2003-04
2004-05
2005-06
2006-07
2007-08
Deposits
Outstanding Advances

and outstanding advances rose to Rs. 63,456.79 and Rs. 27,980.98 crores respectively in 2007-08.

Credit Policy for Agricultural Development

Agricultural credit is one of the most crucial inputs in all agricultural development programmes for a long time. The major source of agricultural credit was the private money-lenders, this source of credit was inadequate and highly expensive and exploitative.[13]

The All India Rural Credit Survey (1951-52). All India Rural Credit Review Committee 1966, and several Economists have pointed out several defects in the working and organisation of cooperative credit society has been considered as the best agency to finance agriculture since 1904 to 1969. The posing of the Cooperative Society Act, 1904 led to the publication of the report of the All India Rural Credit Review Committee.

Multi Agency Approach to Finance Agriculture

During 1966, there was major development in the field of agriculturist it was result of adoption of new agriculture technology and HYVP. The green revolution opened up for the first time entirely new vistas of agrarian development. It become evident that agricultural production could be increased in a relatively short time, if adequate inputs made available. The availability of inputs like irrigation, HYV seeds and fertilizers, pesticides, insecticides etc., were possible only with the help of large investments. These investments could be made. Only if the peasantry was to be assured of adequate and easy credit arrangement.[14]

In view of increasing requirements of agricultural credit, the government accepted the multi-agency approach to finance agriculture.

In the earlier policy, before 1968, there was an exclusive dependence on the cooperative to disabuses agricultural credit commercial banks were more or less stunned. Since 1970

India come to practice what has come to be known as the multi-agency approach in the rural credit. At present many agencies are significantly operating in the field of agricultural finance, such as cooperative credit societies, commercial banks, lead banks, RRBs, etc.

The multi-agency approach came to be adopted as the overall national policy as no single complex financial institution has the necessary organizational structure of financial strengths to cater to the total requirements of the Indian agriculture.

Recommendations of Kamath Working Group (1976)

The Reserve Bank of India constituted a working group under the chairmanship of C.E.Kamath in Aug 1976 to study the problems arising out of the adoption of multi-agency approach in agricultural financing and make appropriate recommendations.

The Kamath Committee recommended regional approach for branch expansion whereby one or two banks with strong base is given the responsibility of opening branches in unbanked rural regions. This would make it possible for bank officials to inspect and also supervisions a large number of forms in a single visit, which will make supervision more effective and also reduce the cost of inspection and supervision of agricultural advances.

This scheme was introduced in 1972. On the recommendations of RBI committee under the chairmanship of Dr. R.K. Hazari the categories of eligible borrowers under DIR scheme were landless labourers. Small landsholders, rural artisans, etc.

Regional Rural Banks and Agriculture Credit in India

The credit requirements of cultivators for agricultural purpose are met by institutional as well as non-institutional agencies. They later include agriculturist, money-lenders, merchants and commission agents. The institutional agencies that lend money to cultivators are cooperative, government commercial banks, regional rural banks, etc.

Until, 1968 the official policy was to develop the co-operative system as the sole agency for meeting agricultural credit requirements. But the All India Rural Credit Review Committee (1969) pointed out that cooperatives are not adequately meeting the credit requirement of agriculture, the fact brought commercial banks into the field of agricultural credit.[15] The single agency approach has changed into multi-agency approach to agricultural finance. However commercial banks could not come to expectations, commercial banks faced following problems.

The small and marginal formers were felt high and dry without any benefit from massive amount flowing into the agricultural sectors.

Thus this gave the birth to regional rural banks in 1975 mainly to bring the gap felt unfilled due to the failure of cooperative banks on the one hand and commercial banks on the other in disseminating adequate credit to the agricultural sector in particular.

Thus the president on 26th Sep., 1975 promulgated the Regional Rural Banks ordinance. Which come into force with immediate effect. The main objective of setting up of the RRBs was to provide credit and other facilities especially to small and marginal farmers, agricultural labourers in rural areas.

In practice the RRBs are required to undertake granting loans and advances to small scales and marginal farmers and agricultural labours whether individually or in-groups of cooperative societies or farmers services societies for agricultural purpose or agricultural operations or related purposes.

RRBs and Agricultural Development in India

Regional Rural Banks in India are directly and indirectly supporting agricultural development in numerous ways. RRBs

Table 3.9
RRBs Loans to Agricultural Development Purpose

(Amount in lakhs)

Purpose-wise classification	*2003-04*	*2004-05*	*2005-06*	*2006-07*	*2007-08*
1. Agriculture Crop Loans	20808.29 (19.25)	2204428 80206.71 (17.33)	2170289 88666.68 (16.87)	2286769 111508.88 (17.72)	2322671 130824.90 (17.40)
2. Agriculture term loans	23079.63 (21.35)	1856610 79820.59 (17.25)	89418.25 1752094 (17.02)	10669142 103973.17 (16.52)	1652971 123450.10 (16.40)
3. Agriculture and allied activities	20519.03 (18.99)	2194326 67428.02 (14.57)	2252309 77891.96 (14.82)	2201590 85408.30 (13.57)	2170486 92376.30 (12.30)
4. Non-agriculture loans	31521.62 (29.17)	4766438 16789885.23 (36.28)	4618844 181261.44 (34.50)	4535417 207849.66 (33.03)	4631465 242279.16 (32.20)
5. Others	12148.59 (11.29)	13600[illegible] 67732.17 (14.55)	1628867 88064.01 (16.72)	1904972 120354.29 (19.13)	1881772 161572.08 (21.52)
6. Total	1,08,077.15 (100)	12381852 462672.72	12422403 525302.34	12597890 629095.96	12659365 750302.54

Sources: National Bank for Agriculture and Rural Development (NABARD) Statistics on Regional Rural Banks, 2007-08.
Note: Number of beneficiaries.

give agricultural term loans for land based activities, such as minor irrigation, drip irrigation, to purchase tractors, tillers so that there will be increase in productivity by using modern skills and technology, so that there will be agricultural development.

RRBs also help agricultural development by giving crop loans, crops are advanced with the object of providing financial assistance to small and marginal formers to purchase seeds, chemical fertilizers and manure particulars.[16] Crop loans are production-oriented loans and help in raising the crop to agriculture development by giving loans to allied activities. Table 3.9 indicates the regional rural banks loans to agricultural development since 2003-04 to 2007-08.

Now let us discuss in detail RRBs advances to the development of agriculture in India. In the year 2003-04, the total loan disbursed was Rs. 1,08,077.15 lakh. During December 2003 the share of crop loans was 19.25% with Rs.20,808.29 lakh worth of loans. In the same year, the share of agriculture term loans was 21.35% with Rs.23,079.63 lakh worth of credit. The share of allied activities was 18.99% with Rs. 20,519.03 lakh worth of credit.

In the year 2004-05, the total loan disbursed amount to 462672.72 lakhs benefiting 1238152 beneficiaries. During March 2004 the share of crop loans slightly decreased from 19.25% to 17.33% benefiting 2204428 beneficiaries with Rs. 80206.71 lakhs worth of loans.

In the year 2004-05 the share of agriculture term loans decreased to 17.25% benefiting 1856610 beneficiaries with Rs. 79,820.59 lakh worth of loans. The share of allied activities was a 14.57% beneficiary 2194326 with Rs. 67428.02 lakh worth of loans.

In the year 2005-06, the total loan disbursed amount to Rs.5,25,302.34 lakh benefiting 1,24,22,403 beneficiaries. During 2004 the share of crop loans decreased to 16.87% benefiting 2170289 beneficiaries with Rs. 88,666.68 lakh worth of loans. The share of term loans remained same at 17.2% but benefiting

1752094 beneficiaries with Rs. 89418.25 lakh worth of loans. The share of allied activities was also same at 14.82% benefiting 22,52,309 beneficiaries with Rs. 77891.96 lakhs worth of loans.

In the year 2006-07, the total loan disbursed amount to Rs.6,29,095.96 lakh benefiting 1,25,97,890 beneficiaries. During March 2007, the share of crop loans increased slightly to 17.72% with Rs. 1,11,508.88 lakh worth of credit benefiting 22,86,769 members.

The share of term loans decreased slightly to 16.52% with Rs. 1,03,973.17 lakh worth of credit benefiting 1,06,69,142 members. The share of allied activities was 13.57% with Rs. 85408.30 lakh worth of credit benefiting 22,01,590 beneficiaries.

During the year 2007-08, the total loan disbursed to Rs. 7,50,302.54 lakh benefiting 1,26,59,365 beneficiaries. During March 2007 the share of crop loans was 17.40% with Rs.1,30,824.90 lakhs worth of credit, benefiting 23,22,671 members. The share of term loans slightly decreased to 16.4% with Rs. 1,23,450.10 lakh benefiting 16,52,971 members. The share of allied activities decreased to 12.3% with Rs. 92,376.30 lakhs benefiting 21,70,486.

Regional Rural Banks and the Rural Poor

RRBs were created to have targetted lending in the rural areas. The performance of RRBs over the years has not been great. In the past few years the RRBs have turned around from their extended state of sickness. Even so, the loans as a per centage of resources at their command (Credit - Deposit Ratio) are falling but for an improvement is 2003. The ratio of RRBs should be compared to the commercial banks over the years. The commercial banks and CD ratio of 60% as against the CD ratio and RRBs ratio of 40%. This means that the turnaround story of the RRBs has been at the cost of access to credit to rural areas. In the years where the deployment of credit was high (1997) the NPAs were also high at 36.81% and the system as a whole was incurring losses. The NPA ratio has consistently fallen in the past years and now it is time for RRBs to get back to their basic business of lending. This co-insides with a stable low interest rate regime and therefore opportunities for arbitrage in the money market and interest earnings from investments, which were a major source of income in the past years, are going to have limited impact on bottom lines of the RRBs. However that fact is that RRBs provide an outlet for the rural people for save.

Table 3.10
Results of RRBs over the Years

(Rs. Crores)

Details	*2001-02*	*2002-03*	*2003-04*	*2004-05*	*2005-06*	*2006-07*	*2007-08*
Resources Mobilised	16971	20978	26319	31306	38696	44873	50190
Loans Out-standing	8718	9692	11356	13109	15794	19075	22585
Interest income	6606	2014	3286	3895	4625	5191	5501
Other income	87	107	157	205	234	372	430
Operating Profits	(53)	133	335	530	730	774	714
Net Profits	(589)	76	247	428	600	608	524
CD Profits	50.3	46.2	43.3	42.14	42.07	42.51	45.00
Invest-ment Deposit Ratio	14.66	16.82	19.69	20.00	20.38	15.67	25.90
Standard Assets	63.2	67.2	72.2	76.9	81.2	83.9	NO
Non-Performing Assets	36.8	32.8	27.8	23.1	18.8	16.1	NO

Source : Trend and Progress of Banking in India RBI (various years).

In the past several measures were taken to improve the performance of the RRBs these included a programme of recapitalisation to the extent of Rs. 2,188 crore examining of merger of RRBs sponsored by the same bank and closing of non-profitable branches. In addition they have been encouraged to issue Kisan CreditCards and use micro-finance as a mechanism to reach the poor by encouraging them to promote and lend to SHGs. The de-regulation of interest rates has gone a long way in making RRBs competitive and market survey. In 2002, a working group also submitted a report recommending changes in the RRB Act which if implemented would change significant aspects of operations of the RRBs.[17]

Although the progress of the RRBs is commendable, still there are certain gaps in their functioning. It is found that the credit channelised through the institutional agencies is less than the requirement. In spite of widespread bank expansion, there are still under-banked areas. The gap between the demand for and supply of the credit from existing institutional agencies is wide. While the cooperatives are democratic institutions, the commercial banks, and even the RRBs are bureaucratic institutions. They are not likely to succeed in enticing the cooperation of the rural public and commanding their support and participation.[18]

Loans and Advances to Priority Sectors

The performance of the banks in meeting the credit needs under agriculture, total priority advances has to be increased to Rs. 20,63,235.7 lakhs compared to Rs. 7,14,269.92 lakhs in the year 2003-04. The growth amount is Rs. 13,48,965.8 lakh. It is a good signal to agriculture, which is the main occupation of India. In state-wise disbursement of loans and advances, Uttar Pradesh state issued highest amount of advances i.e., Rs.3,66,779.10 lakh as on 31-03-2006. Andhra Pradesh has been provided Rs. 3,39,531.80 lakh of loans to priority sectors. This is the second state being provided the highest amount to priority sectors. Year-wise and state-wise disbursement of loans and advances to priority sector is furnished hereunder.

Table 3.11
Priority Sector Advances [Year-wise]

Sectors	*2003-04*	*2004-05*	*2005-06*	*2006-07*	*2007-08*
Total Priority Sector	714269.9	884660.8	1172230.2	1656802	2063235.7
Short Term (Crop Loan)	381161.7	483374.1	613291.01	988343.9	1281589.4
Term Loan (Agri & Allied)	78195.9	104531.1	104206.05	204339.7	248362.93
Rural Artisans	19807.17	23829.06	27621.97	31642.72	30619.72
Small Scale Industries	10671.97	13846.26	16713.56	20961.36	28072.45
Retail Trade Etc	127924	142123.1	165315.35	196669.2	162447.17
SHGs	18012.14	35019.23	50953.62	85849.75	102481.43
Others	78497.05	81938.06	194128.63	128995.9	209662.62

Source : Annual Reports of NABARD.

Since the RRBs are satisfying to a large extent all the conditions of a sound rural credit system in the context of problem hidden area, it is desirable to take necessary steps by the Government of India for their expansion in a large scale. [19]

The main problems in a case of cooperatives and Regional Rural Banks (RRBs) which supply bulk of the short-terms production credit to agriculture were higher interest rates on deposits, lower interest rates on advances, higher operating costs because of small loans, which were advanced exclusively to the weaker sections in backward areas and higher default rates.

The most common problems with rural credit have been defective loan policies, delays in sanction and disbursement of loans and fixation of due dates, which were not compatible with the harvesting and marketing seasons.

At times, the loan among was not even enough to fulfill the entire needs of the borrowers, which compelled them to borrow from local money-lenders or other informal sources. In such a situation, the amount borrower from money-lenders obviously received a higher priority in the repayment plan of the borrowers.[20]

Under the old system, short-term credit was disbursed either through a demand loan known as crop cash credit mechanism. In the demand loan based system, loans were granted on crop specific basis against execution of fresh documents each season. Some banks followed the crop cash credit mechanism under which borrowers were sanctioned sub-limits within an aggregate limit on the basis of standard criteria such as cropping pattern, scale of finance and land-holding. When the sub-limit was fully used up only credits were permitted, but withdrawals under these limits were permitted either in cash through debit slips or through banker's cheques for the kind component. As a result the withdrawals were usually bunched at the beginning of crop season and repayments at the end of the season when farmers were able to generate cash after harvesting and marketing their produce.

Thus, the main weaknesses of the erstwhile system of short-term credit delivery were following. Firstly for each crop, farmers were required to file separate application and complete all formalities for obtaining loans, which obviously involved a lot of paper work. Secondly, the system did not allow farmers to use credit limits as a regular cash credit for meeting their production requirements as and when they wanted. Thirdly, farmers were also required to submit a no due certificate each time while taking fresh loans. There are a large number of studies, which indicate that farmers in developing countries are credit constrained.

Further, most common reasons for overdues in the past were inadequacy of sanctioned loan amount due to ad hoc and unrealistic limits, scale of finance and delays in sanctions and disbursements of loans.

Agricultural Credit: Discernible Trends

In India a multi-agency approach comprising Cooperative banks, scheduled commercial banks and RRBs has been followed for purveying credit to agricultural sector. The policy of agricultural credit is guided mainly by the considerations of ensuring adequate and timely availability of credit at reasonable rates through the expansion of institutional framework, its outreach and scale as also by way of directed lending. Over time, spectacular progress has been achieved in terms of the scale and outreach of institutional framework for agricultural credit. Some of the major discernible trends are as follows:

1. Over time the public sector banks have made commendable progress in terms of putting in place a wide banking network, particularly in the aftermath of nationalization of banks. The number of offices of public sector banks increased rapidly from 8,262 in June 1969 to 68,355 by March 2005.
2. One of the major achievements in the post-independent India has been widening the spread of institutional machinery for credit and decline in the role of non-institutional sources, notwithstanding some reversal in the trend observed particularly in the 1990s.
3. The share of institutional credit, which was little over 7 per cent in 1951, increased manifold to over 66 per cent in 1991, reflecting concomitantly a remarkable decline in the share of non-institutional credit from around 93 per cent to about 31 per cent during the same period. However, the latest NSSO survey reveals that the share of no-institutional credit has taken a reverse swing which is a cause of concern (Table 3.12).

Table 3.12
Relative Share of Borrowing of Cultivator Households from Different Sources

Sources of Credit	*1951*	*1961*	*1971*	*1981*	*1991*	*2002*
Non-institutional	92.7	81.3	68.3	36.8	30.6	38.9
Of which Money-Lenders	69.7	49.2	36.1	16.1	17.5	26.8
Institutional	7.3	18.7	31.7	63.2	66.3	61.1
Of which3.3 Cooperative banks		2.6	22.0	29.8	23.6	30.2
Commercial banks	0.9	0.6	2.4	28.8	35.2	26.3
Unspecified	-	-	-	-	3.1	-
Total	100.0	100.0	100.0	100.0	100.0	100.0

Source: All India Debt and Investment Survey and NSSO.

1. Notwithstanding their wide network, cooperative banks, particularly since the 1990s have lost their dominant position to commercial banks. The share of cooperative banks (22%) during 2005-06 was less than half of what it was in 1992-93 (62%), while the share of commercial banks (33 to 68%) including RRBs (5 to 10%) almost doubled during the above period (figures).
2. The efforts to increase the flow of credit to agriculture seems to have yielded better results in the recent period as the total institutional credit to agriculture recorded a growth of around 21 per cent during 1995-96 to 2004-05 from little over 12 per cent during 1986-87 to 1994-95. In terms of total credit to agriculture, the commercial banks recorded a considerable growth (from around 13 per cent to

about 21 per cent), while cooperative banks registered a fall (over 14% to over 10%) during the above period).

3. However, the growth of direct finance to agriculture and allied activities witnessed a decline in the 1990s (12%) as compared to the 1980s (14%) and 1970s (around 16 per cent). Furthermore, a comparative analysis of direct credit to agriculture and allied activities during 1980s and since 1990s reveals the fact that the average share of long-term credit in the total direct finance has not only been much lower but has also decelerated (from over 38% to around 36%), which could have dampening effect on the agricultural investment for future growth process.
4. The disaggregated picture as per size-wise distribution of credit reveals that the growth of direct finance to small and marginal farmers witnessed a marked deceleration from about 24 per cent in the 1980s to little over 13 per cent during the 1990s.
5. Sectoral deployment of gross bank credit reveals that the share of agriculture since the second half of 1990s has ranged between 11 – 12 per cent. As at the end March 2006, the share stood at around 11.9 per cent.

Recent Policy Initiatives

The Finance Minister in his Union Budget 1995-96 speech stated that, "Inadequacy of public investment in agriculture is today a matter of general concern. This is an area which is the responsibility of states. But many states have neglected investment in infrastructure for agriculture. There are many rural infrastructure projects which have been started but are lying incomplete for want of resources. They represent a major loss of potential income and employment to rural population".

Rural Infrastructure Development Fund (RIDF) was set up in NABARD. Since then, 11 branches of allocations have been made towards the Fund. Commercial banks make contribution towards the fund on account of the shortfalls in their priority/agriculturesector lending. The scope of RIDF has been widened to enable utilization of loan by Panchayati Raj Institutions (PRIs), Self-Help Groups (SHGs), Non-Governmental Organizations (NGOs), etc., since 1999-2000.

The fund has continued with additional corpus being announced every year in the Union Budget. The RIDF XI was announced in the Union Budget for 2005-06 with an allocation of Rs. 8,000 crore making a total corpus of Rs. 50,000 crore. RIDF XI accorded special emphasis for setting up of village knowledge centres by providing Rs. 100 crore out of the corpus of Rs. 8,000 crore.

Two innovations, viz., micro-finance and Kisan Credit Card Scheme have emerged as the major policy developments in addressing the infirmities associated with the distributional aspects of credit in the recent years. The KCC schenme has emerged as the most effective mode of credit delivery to agriculture in terms of the timeliness, hassle-free operations as also adequacy of credit with minimum of transaction costs and documentation.

Summary

Policy on agriculture credit aims at progressive institutionalization of credit agencies for providing credit to farmers for raising agricultural production and productivity. Agricultural credit is disbursed through a multi-agency network consisting of cooperatives, commercial banks and RRBs. The 'Farm Credit Package' announced in June 2004 stipulated doubling the flow of institutional credit for agriculture in the ensuing years. The credit flow to farm sector got doubled during two years as against the stipulated time period of three years. During 2006-07 the total institutional credit flow to agriculture sector was Rs. 2,03,297 crore having shares of cooperative banks, RRBs and commercial banks at 20.9%, 10.1% and 69% respectively. Government has decided that from Kharif 2006-07, farmers would receive crop loans up to a principal amount of Rs.3

lakh at 7 per cent rate of interest. During 2007-08, the government of India is providing interest subvention of 2 per cent per annum to public sector banks, regional rural banks and cooperative banks on amount of short term agriculture credit disbursed out of their own resources.

References

1. Rani Ratna Prabha (2008): *Agricultural Credit in India in Pre- and Post-reform Period,* Southern Economist, vol. 47, No.12 October. Bangalore.
2. Gupta, V.S. (2002): *Agriculture in India: A Saga of Rapid Growth,* Sage Publications, New Delhi.
3. Bhalla, G.S. and Gurmail Singh (2001): *Indian Agriculture – Four Decades of Development,* Sage Publications, New Delhi.
4. Patel M.C and S.M.Pillai (2006): *The Importance of Agriculture and Growth Rate of Agricultural Sector during the Post-Reforms Period,* Yojana, Vol. 45, New Delhi.
5. Rajasekhar, D. and Gagan Bihari Sahu (2007) "Expansion at the Expense of Equity- Institutional Credit Flow to Agriculture in Karnataka" in Rural Karnataka edited by Jayasheela, Serials Publications, New Delhi.
6. Alexandros, Nicos (1993): Agriculture Towards 2010, Rome: Food and Agriculture Organisation of United Nations.
7. Datt Ruddar and Sundaram K.P.M (2003): "Indian Economy", S.Chand & Company Ltd., New Delhi.
8. Reddy Y.V (2004), *Rural Credit: Status and Agenda,* RBI Bulletin, December, pp. 1087-1089.
9. Varde, S.V., "Quantitative Dimension of Rural Banking", PRAJNAN, Vol. XIII, No.1, (Jan- Mar. 1985), pp. 137-50.
10. Wadhwa, Subhas, C., Banking of the Poor, for the Poor and by the Poor, Financial Express, Bangalore, (Nov. 17, 1992).
11. Thingalaya, N.K., "Agricultural Credit and Recovery; Some Issues", *Pigmy Economic Review,* monthly Economic Journal of Syndicate Bank, Vol. 34, No.6, (Jan., 1989).
12. Shete, N.B. "Experience of Agricultural Loan Recoveries in some Developing Countries; Lesson for Indian Commercial

Bank", *PRAJNAN*, Vol. XXI, No.1, (Jan- Mar., 1992), pp. 89-102.

13. Rath, Neelkanth, "Institutional Credit for Agriculture in India", *Journal of Indian School of Political Economy,* Vol.1, No.2, (Jul-Dec., 1989).
14. Rath, Neelkanth, "Agricultural Growth and Investment in India", *Journal of the Indian School of Political Economy,* Vol. 1, No.1, (Jan- Jun. 1989).
15. Patel, K.V. "Farm Sector Credit and Rural Banking", *Economic Times,* Bombay, (Jun. 4, 1990).
16. Khemari, C.L., "Area Approach in Agricultural lending", State Bank of India, *Monthly Review,* Vol. XX. No.1, (Jan,1981). pp. 32-36.
17. Kaul, R.K., "Role of Banks in Uplifting People above the Line of Poverty" *PRAJNAN,* Vol. X, No.2 Vol.X, No.2 (Apr- Jun., 1981). PP. 127-34.
18. Joshi, P.N., "Banking in Rural India", *The Journal of India Institute Bankers,* Vol. 40. No. 1, (Jan- Mar., 1969).
19. Hutchappa, G.T., "Commercial Banks and Agricultural Finance", *The Asian Economic Review,* Vol. X, No. 3, (May 1968).
20. Dandekar, V.N. and Wadia, F.K. "Development of Institutional Credit for Agriculture in India", *Journal of Indian School of Political Economy,* Vol. 1, No. 2 (Jan-Dec., 1989).

4

Performance of Regional Rural Banks in Karnataka: An Analysis

Introduction

This chapter analyses the origin and growth of Grameena Banks in Karnataka, branch expansion of grameena banks in Karnataka, credit deployment and advances to various sectors in the state economy. Analysis starts with brief introduction of the regional rural banks.

Regional Rural banks in Karnataka have come a long way since 1976, when the first grameen bank in the state was established. Since then twelve more grameen banks were sponsored, covering all the districts in the state. Passing through critical periods, when their very survival was doubtful, they have marched to a stage of revival. Compared to those operating in different states, these banks have proved to be viable rural credit agencies accessible to the weaker sections of society. Two of them have proved to be role models — Malaprabha Grameena Bank and Tungabhadra Grameena Bank. Incidentally, when the Government of India initiated the process of reorganisation of Grameena Banks in September 2005, these two banks were the first banks, with whom six other Grameen Banks in the State were emerged.

Collectively, the Grameena Banks constitute a sizeable part of the rural banking base in the state.

It is the interest evinced by the banks in the state that is responsible for the growth and spread of Grameena Banks in Karnataka. The five public sector banks originating from the state and the omnipresent big brother – State Bank of India have sponsored thirteen Grameena Banks in the state. The state government has also taken keen interest in their formation, as a minor partner, the Government of India being the major shareholder.

Growth and Spread of Regional Rural Banks

Impatient was the Government of India in boosting the rural banking sector after bank nationalization, not satisfied with the progress made in this direction by the nationalised banks. An alternative, farmer friendly, rural-oriented, low cost rural credit agency was considered necessary to meet the rural credit requirements. The Government of India appointed a working group in 1975 under the chairmanship of M. Narasimham to examine in depth the setting up of new rural banks as subsidiaries of public sector banks. In the appointment letter, the Ministry of Finance has emphasised, "that unless new institutions are started on the basis of attitudinal and operational ethos entirely different from those obtaining in the public sector banks, we shall only be perpetuating the present mode of function in the public sector banking system". Before the recommendations were operationalised by an Act of the Parliament, two public sector banks were asked to sponsor the new rural banks in Uttar Pradesh. An ordinance was passed to pave the way for their establishment in 1975. The Regional Rural Banks Act, 1976 was passed later, making the Government of India, the state governments of the states concerned and the public sector banks as the shareholders. The Government of India was to hold 50 per cent of the capital, State government 15 per cent and the sponsoring bank to hold 35 per cent. Public sector banks started the process of establishing grameena banks in their lead districts.

Canara Bank sponsored the first grameena bank in Karnataka, Tungabhadra Grameena Bank in 1976, at Bellary, covering Bellary and Raichur districts. It was named after the river, which was irrigating a vast portion of the command area of this bank. During the same year, Syndicate Bank established Malaprabha Grameena Bank at Dharwad, covering Dharwad and Belgaum districts. Malaprabha river is a tributary of Krishna river flowing in these two districts. Cauvery Grameena Bank also came in to being in the same year at Mysore sponsored by State Bank of Mysore. Cauvery river, historically, has been an integral part of the socio-economic life of the old Mysore state. The area of operation of this bank was the two districts of Mysore and Hassan.

Krishna Grameena Bank, named after the mighty Krishna river was born in Gulbarga in 1978, sponsored by the State Bank of India, covering Gulbarga and Bidar districts. Canara Bank sponsored the next grameen bank, Chitradurga Grameena Bank in 1981 at Chitradurga, a town of historical importance. Kalpatharu Grameena Bank, sponsored by State Bank of Mysore appeared at Tumkur in 1982. It was named after the cash crop predominantly grown in the district—Kalpatharu, the coconut tree.

In 1983, Kolar witnessed the birth of Kolar Grameena Bank. Canara Bank, which perhaps found it appropriate to name it after the town, promoted it known for the gold mines. During the same year, Syndicate Bank sponsored Bijapur Grameena Bank at Bijapur, the historical town, where the Golgumbaz stands even to this date as a reminder of the Bahamani rulers.

Corporation Bank took up the sponsorship of Chikamagalur-Kodagu Grameena Bank in 1984. Covering the two districts, its headquarter was in Chikamagalur. Its lengthy name is now abridged into Chiko Grameena Bank. In Shimoga, the small town tucked in the Sahyadri mountain range, Canara Bank established Sahyadri Grameena Bank. This was followed by Netravathi Grameena Bank of syndicate Bank, at Mangalore. River Netravati flows from the Western Ghats to join the sea at Mangalore. The fourth bank to be born in the same year was Varada Grameena Bank at Kumta. Syndicate Bank chose to name it after a small, less known river that flows in Uttara Kannada district.

Table 4.1
Grameena Banks in Karnataka

Sl. No	*Name of the Bank*	*Location*	*Year*	*Sponsoring Bank*
01.	Tungabhadra Grameena Bank	Bellary	1976	Canara Bank
02.	Malaprabha Grameena Bank	Dharwad	1976	Syndicate Bank
03.	Cauvery Grameena Bank	Mysore	1976	State Bank of Mysore
04.	Krishna Grameena Bank	Gulbarga	1978	State Bank of India
05.	Chitradurga Grameena Bank	Chitradurga	1981	Canara Bank
06.	Kalpatharu Grameena Bank	Tumkur	1982	State Bank of Mysore
07.	Kolar Grameena Bank	Kolar	1983	Canara Bank
08.	Bijapur Grameena Bank	Bijapur	1983	Syndicate Bank
09.	Chikmagalur - Kodagu Gameena Bank	Chikmagalur	1984	Corporation Bank
10.	Sahyadri Grameena Bank	Shimoga	1984	Canara Bank
11.	Netravati Grameena Bank	Mangalore	1984	Syndicate Bank
12.	Varada Grameena Bank	Kumta	1984	Syndicate Bank
13.	Visweshwaraiah Grameena Bank	Mandya	1985	Vijaya Bank

Source: NABARD Reports, Various Issues, Bangalore.

The last grameen bank to come up in the state was Visveshvaraya Grameena Bank at Mandya in 1985. Very thoughtfully it was named after Sir M. Visveshvaraya, the well-known engineer - statesman, who was the architect of the irrigational facilities, ushering in prosperity to Mandya district.

As purveyors of rural credit, these banks have been very effective in extending credit facilities to large number of rural households. They have opened branches in many inaccessible villages and tribal villages. They have been able to bring to the banking fold small borrowers in good number, inculcating in them banking habits. Initially, these banks were directed to confine their business to the targets groups – the marginal farmers, agricultural labourers and village artisans, lending at relatively lower rates of interest. This factor has adversely affected their profit earning capacity. Conceived as a low cost credit agency, its pay scales were on par with that of the local government staff, lower than that of the bank staff. The wage revision made to bring about wage- parity as a result of the labour dispute raised the wage bill substantially, pushing many banks into red. It is only after liberalization and de-regulation of their customer-base, many of them could move back into good health.

The total number of branches of grameen banks in Karnataka is 1148. These branches constitute 53 per cent of the rural banking base of bank in the state. Handling over 43 lakh deposit account, they mobilize 36 per cent of the total deposits mobilized by the rural branches of all banks. Grameena banks service about 54 per cent of the rural customers. Out of every rupee lent by banks in the rural sector in Karnataka, Grameen Banks disburse 40 paise.

Poor recovery was the bane of a few Grameen Banks during the last few years. Now they have geared up their recovery machinery and are on par with the commercial banks in this sphere. With high NPA ratios, some of them were in the red for some time. Grameen banks in the state have proved their viability as all of them are now earning profits. The accumulated losses have been wiped out over the years. (N.K. Thingalaya, 2006).

Area of Operation

Small size of the area of operation of many grameen banks was one of the limiting factors. Some of them were confined to single districts or a couple of districts. The Government of India has decided to merge the grameen banks at the state level on a selective basis. The sponsoring banks were directed to merge their grameen banks operating within the states. This process was begun in September 2005. Three of the sponsoring banks have already implemented this process of revitalizing grameen banks.

Syndicate Bank has merged four of its grameen banks – Malaprabha Grameena Bank, Varada Grameena Bank, Netravati Grameena Bank and Bijapur Grameena Bank into Karnataka Vikasa Grameena Bank. The new bank has a network of 387 branches, spread out in 9 districts; Dharwad, Belguam, Bagalkote, Bijapur, Gadag, Haveri, Uttara Kannada, Dakshina Kannada and Udupi. Its deposits are Rs.1917 crore and advances of Rs.1749 crore as on March 2006. It has earned a profit of Rs.32.09 crore. It emerges as one of the biggest grameen banks in India. Its head office is the former head office building of Malaprabha Grameena Bank at Dharwad. This bank has become the first grameen bank in the country to install an ATM. It has a programme of installing 20 ATMs during the current year.

Canara Bank has merged four grameen banks – Tungabhadra Grameena Bank, Chitradurga Grameena Bank, Sahyadri Grameena Bank and Kolar Grameena Bank to form Pragathi Grameena Bank, with its head office in Bellary. This amalgamated bank has a deposit base of Rs.1643 crore and advances of Rs.1614 crore. Covering 7 districts – Bellary, Raichur, Koppal, Kolar, Davanagere, Shimoga and Chitradurga, it has 350 branches.

Cauvery Grameena Bank and Kalpatharu Grameena Bank

sponsored by State Bank of Mysore have been merged and renamed as Cauvery Kalpatharu Grameena Bank from June 29, 2006. Operating in six districts – Mysore, Hassan, Chamarajanagar, Tumkur, Bangalore – rural and Bangalore - urban district, it has 202 branches. The deposits of the amalgamated bank are Rs. 798 crore and advances are Rs. 605 crore.

With this, the number of Grameena Banks in the state has come down from 13 to 6. The other three grameen banks operating now in the state are : Krishna Grameena Bank sponsored by State Bank of India; Chikamagalur - Kodagu Grameena Bank sponsored by Corporation Bank and Visveshwarayya Grameena Bank, sponsored by Vijaya Bank. Since sponsors of these three grameen banks have only one grameen bank each in the state, they are likely to maintain their individual existence.

Grameen banks in the state has already acquired a strategic space in the rural banking segment. They provide a dependable financial infrastructure spread over the entire state. They have built-up expertise in rural banking over the last 30 years. In any of the developmental activities to be introduced in rural India, they can be effectively used. Financial inclusion is now receiving the attention of the planners very seriously. Self-Help Groups are considered as a means for reaching out to the poor, who are yet to be touched by the organized banking sector.

Grameen banks may be considered as one of the most suitable financial agencies for promoting and fostering Self-Help Groups as a conduit for extending micro-finance in rural India. Rural banking being their core-competence, they could be major players in this arena in the future banking scenario. Recognizing their strategic position, it is desirable to make them the kingpin in the micro-finance movement.

Grameen banks already have a ready-made rural base, designed for handling the credit delivery system, conducive for small lending. Having branches in remote rural areas, manned by rural – oriented personnel, they have better accessibility to the needy households than any other agency. They are familiar with the rural ethos. These banks have easy access to low cost funds, mobilized through savings bank deposits from rural households. Performance of many of them in this field is remarkable. For example, Karnataka Vikas Grameena Bank has savings bank deposits of Rs. 884 crore as on 2006 which account for 46 per cent of its total deposits.

Table 4.2
Present Status of Grameen Banks in Karnataka

Sl. No.	*Name of the Bank*	*Deposits (Rs.crore)*	*Advances (Rs.crore)*	*Profit (Rs. crore)*	*Branches (number)*
01.	Karnataka Vikas Grameena Bank	1,917	1,750	32.09	387
02.	Pragathi Grameena Bank	1,643	1,614	23.69	350
03.	Cauvery Kalpatharu Grameena Bank	798	605	16.33	202
04.	Krishna Grameena Bank	463	537	14.06	106
05.	Chikamagalu - Kodagu Grameena Bank	126	109	0.22	49
06.	Visweshwaraih Grameena Bank	90	88	-	25

Source: N.K. Thingalaya (Fifty years of Banking Development)

Grameen banks have been dealing with only small borrowers from the beginning. They were precluded from lending to activities other than those pertaining to the prescribed target groups. Nearly 83 per cent of their borrowing accounts are in the advances group of less than Rs.25,000. Micro-finance should not become one more column in their

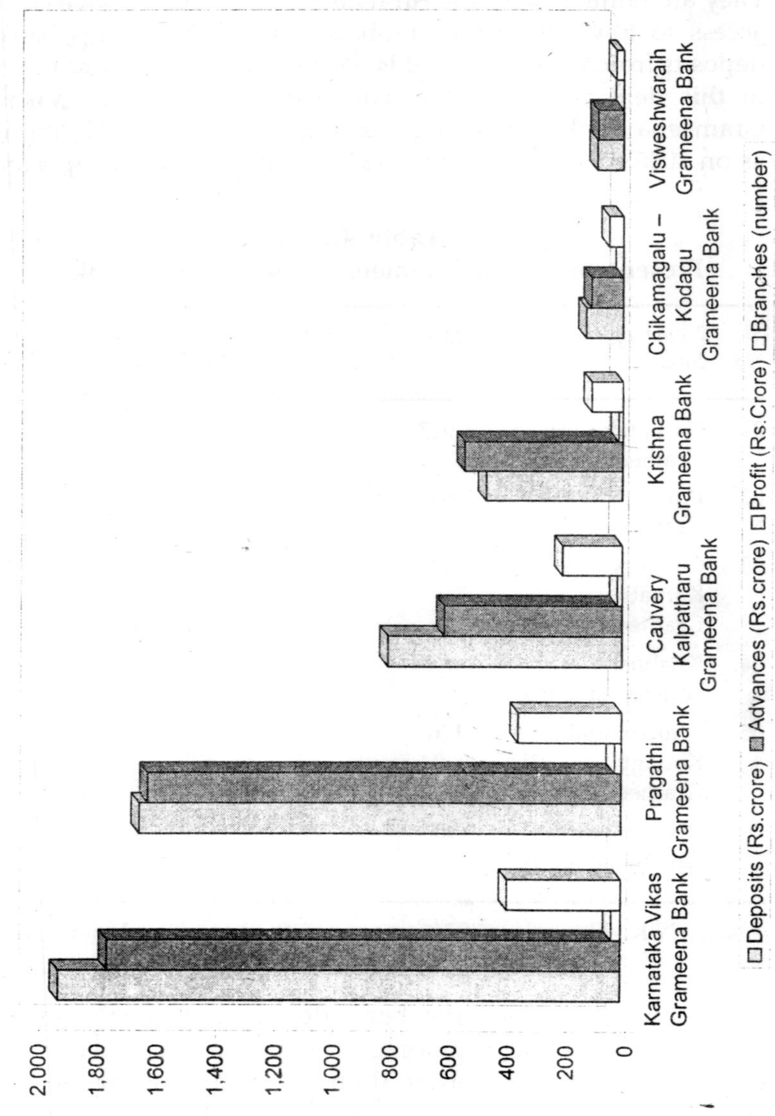
2,000
1,800
1,600
1,400
1,200
1,000
800
600
400
200
0
Karnataka Vikas Grameena Bank
Pragathi Grameena Bank
Cauvery Kalpatharu Grameena Bank
Krishna Grameena Bank
Chikamagalu – Kodagu Grameena Bank
Visweshwaraih Grameena Bank
Deposits (Rs.crore)
Advances (Rs.crore)
Profit (Rs.Crore)
Branches (number)

reporting format. There has been very little effort made to re-orient their lending programmes, assigning the importance due to micro-finance programmes. No doubt, many of them have tried to reach out to the Self-Help Groups to rural women, as reported in their annual reports with photos of some of the beneficiaries, as they are called. But that is not sufficient.

The staff of grameen banks has to be trained in handling micro-finance, with conceptual clarity and understanding operational intricacies. Target fixation has to be avoided. Covering all the households in the villages coming under their jurisdiction, over a reasonable time frame should be the goal. This has to be derived from the methodologically formulated Service Area Credit Plans forming part of the District Credit Plans. They should be built into the branch business plans.

Table 4.3
Total Loans Issued By RRBs in Karnataka

Name of RRB	*2005-06*	*2006-07*	*2007-08*
Bijapur	11366.00	13902.49	17978.76
Cauvery	11693.00	11761.30	15118.13
Chitradurga	12840.46	14258.91	19850.83
Chik-Kodagu	2354.26	3475.57	4396.25
Kalpatharu	7811.14	12299.09	18893.20
Kolar	8008.73	8118.00	10533.00
Krishna	17207.00	17327.00	29505.00
Malaprabha	26125.75	33323.49	44281.24
Netravati	2570.00	3463.32	3689.00
Sahyadri	4169.38	4205.25	5207.10
Tungabadra	45887.00	39210.00	57103.14
Varada	4494.95	6142.06	7125.70
Visveswaraya	3279.17	3761.95	5059.30
Grand Total	157806.84	171248.43	238740.65

Source : Annual Reports of NABARD, various issues.

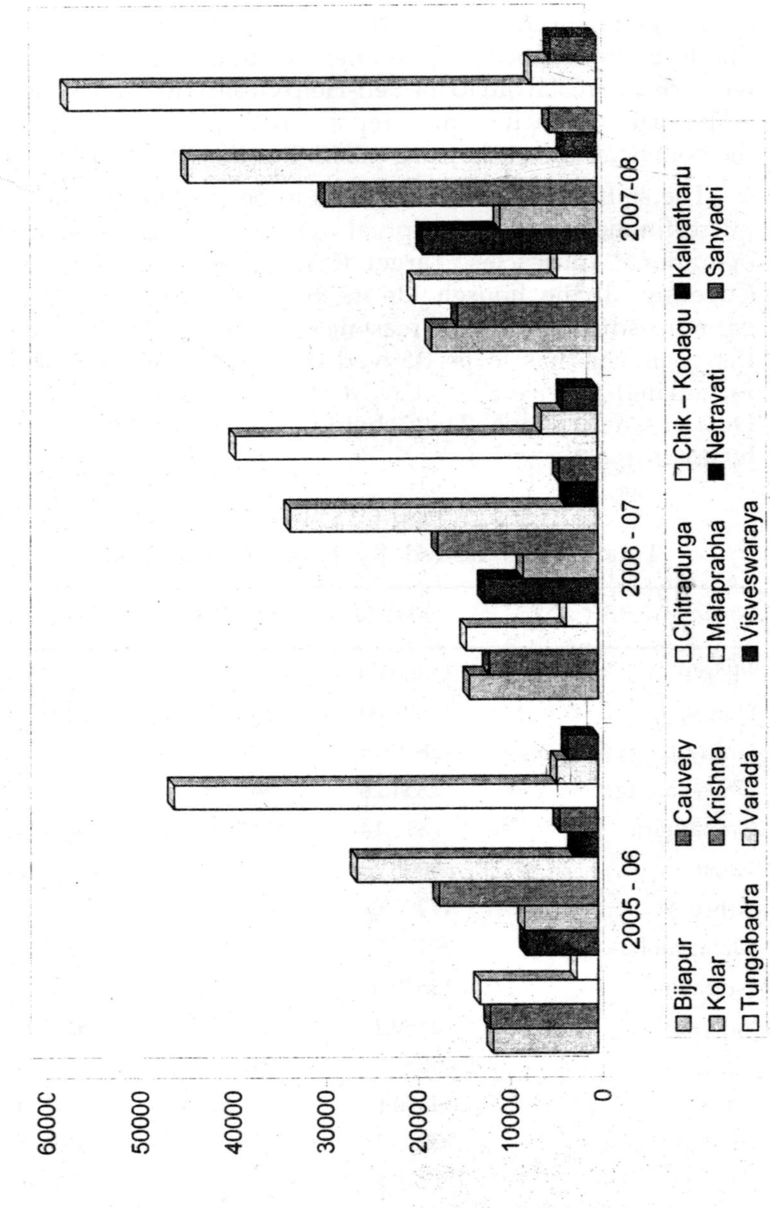
60000
50000
40000
30000
20000
10000
0
2005 - 06
2006 - 07
2007-08
Bijapur
Cauvery
Chitradurga
Chik – Kodagu
Kalpatharu
Kolar
Krishna
Malaprabha
Netravati
Sahyadri
Tungabadra
Varada
Visveswaraya

Organizationally, grameen banks have the handicap of being controlled by three masters, Government of India, Karnataka State Government and the sponsoring bank, while NABARD also comes in as a nodal agency. Granting them the autonomous status is necessary to make them an equal partner in rural banking.

Amalgamation of the rural branches of commercial banks with those of grameen banks at the state-level would be one positive method of consolidating the rural banking structure. It must be admitted that rural banking is not the core competence of commercial banks. They would be willing to withdraw from the rural scene, if permitted by the regulator, who has compelled them to be there. Passing on their rural business to the grameen banks sponsored by them, they can concentrate on core banking business in the non-rural areas from semi-urban to metropolitan areas.

Table 4.4
Share of Grameen Banks in Rural Banking in Karnataka up to 2007-08

Sl. No	*Indicators of Rural Business*	*Grameen Banks*	*All Banks*	*Share of Grameen Banks (per cent)*
01.	Rural Branches (number)	1148	2161	53.12
02.	Deposit Accounts (No.lakh)	43.41	87.07	49.85
03.	Deposit Amount (Rs.crore)	4,102.60	11,393.92	36.00
04.	Borrowing Accounts (No.lakh)	11.81	21.90	53.92
05.	Credit Amount (Rs.crore)	3,759.30	9,255.73	40.61

Source: NABARD, 2007-08.

Privatization of selected grameen banks could be one of the means of making them autonomous and self-reliant. This experiment may be given a trial, asking the highly profitable new generation banks to take over one or two grameen banks.

Managing them as subsidiaries, it could be an organizational challenge to these banks, which often talk about the merger and amalgamation route for their accelerated growth.

The emergent rural banking structure should be financially viable and operationally flexible. Reaching out to the largest number of rural customers, should be the focus, as was enunciated by the authors of the grameen banks. Professionally managed, it should be amenable to the adoption of modern practices. Rural branches should not remain like the village-ration shops, selling only the subsidized products to the selected groups, as the branches of grameen banks have been doing all along. They should evolve themselves as the retail outlets of financial supermarkets, selling the fast moving products at competitive prices and have a strong door-delivery wing for the special customers, SHGs. That some of them have started selling insurance and mutual fund products is a welcome development. Karnataka Vikas Grameena Bank's annual report indicates that the bank has earned a commission of Rs. 24 lakh by selling life insurance and non-life insurance products during 2008.

Status of KCC in Karnataka

In Karnataka, Commercial Banks, Regional Rural Banks and 19 District Central Cooperative Banks are actively engaged in issuing Kisan Credit Cards to farmers. Nearly 23,09,000 Kisan Credit Cards were issued which was 6.3 per cent of the total for all India level as on January 2004. A total credit of Rs.734 crore was issued through KCC which was 8.3 per cent of the total for all India level during the same period.

Out of the total cards issued, cooperative banks, RRBs and commercial banks account for 44.4 per cent, 18.6 per cent and 37 per cent respectively. With regard to cumulative amount sanctioned through KCC, the commercial banks dominate the scene as they account for 43.9 of the total amount sanctioned. The share of cooperative banks and RRBs were 32.3 per cent and 23.8 per cent respectively.

In Karnataka, the ratio of total Kisan Credit Card issued to number of landholdings was 37.1 per cent. The progress therefore, seems to be some what satisfactory.

Status of Kisan Credit Card in Mysore District

The Kisan Credit Card scheme which enables the farmers to obtain loans for their agricultural operations on a revolving cash credit limit basis has been introduced by all the banks with effect from Khariff 1999 season. The Kisan Credit Card scheme basically aims at providing adequate and timely credit support to the farmers for agricultural operations including purchase of inputs.

In the light of the above mentioned issues, it is pertinent to know the impact of KCC on the farming community. How far has the KCC card system helped the farming community in improving their socio-economic conditions? Were the objectives of KCC has fulfilled while delivering the credit facilities? What are the benefits and constraints of this system compared to other credit delivery system? Apart from card-holders, the study will also contact non-cardholders to elicit their opinion on the potential benefits of KCC.

Review of Major Features of KCC Scheme Launched by Commercial Banks

All the 27 public sector commercial banks have launched the Kisan Credit Card Scheme bases on the model scheme circulated by reserve bank of India in August 1998. Barring one or two banks, all public sector commercial banks had prepared their own Kisan Credit Card scheme before December 1998 and launched the scheme on pilot basis in their selected branches. Later on the scheme was expended to cover the entire country.

Eligibility of Farmer for Issue of Kisan Credit Card

Most of the commercial banks had issued KCCs only to those farmers who were having good track record for the last 2-3 years. However, later on, some of the banks have modified these instructions allowing the issue of cards to even new borrowers. Similarly, syndicate bank modified its eligibility criteria to cover all types of farmers and advised all its branches that Kisan Card may be compulsorily issued to all the farmers with requirement of production credit of Rs. 5000 and above.

Minimum Credit Limit

Reserve Bank of India and NABARD while circulating their model scheme on Kisan credit among the banks had recommended Kisan cards for farmers whose requirement of crop loan was 5,000 and above. However, the ceiling was subsequently amended and all the banks were advised that they could workout their own loan limits/ceiling. On a review of the schemes of public sector commercial banks, it is observed that most of the banks have brought down the ceiling from Rs. 5,000 to Rs.3000. Some of the banks did not stipulate any lower ceiling in monetary terms whereas others have prescribed the ceiling in terms of ownership of irrigated land with the farmers, i.e. minimum one acre irrigated land.

Basis for Fixation of Credit Limit

Reserve Bank of India and NABARD through the model scheme circulated amount the banks had recommended that credit limit under Kisan cards may be fixed on the basis of operational landholding, cropping pattern and scales of finance as recommended by District-Level Technical Committee (DLTC) State0-Level Technical Committee (SLTC). Wherever, the DLTC/SLTC have not recommended scale of finance for crops or in the opinion of the bank, recommended lower scales than required amount, banks were allowed to fix appropriate scales of finances for the crop. It was also stipulated that for fixation of credit limit operational land holding might include the leased in land and exclude leased out land. Most of the banks have followed the above guidelines as suggested in the model scheme.

Restriction on Maximum Amount

Except Union Bank of India, Allahabad bank and Punjab National Bank, the public sector commercial banks have not prescribed any maximum limit under Kisan Card.

Fixation of Seasonal Limit

The model scheme had recommended that while fixing the limit, banks may take into account entire production credit requirement for the farmers for full year including the credit requirement of the farmer for ancillary activities related to crop production such as maintenance of agricultural machinery/ implements, electricity charges etc., and also allied activities and non-farm activities. Banks were also advised to fix appropriate sub-limits auctioned, taking into account the seasonally in the credit requirement. The scheme circulated by most of the banks had included this feature in their instructions a few of the banks have built this feature within the methodology adopted for working out the overall limit, while other banks have left it to the discretion of branch managers to fix seasonal limits.

Credit limit of working capital requirement for agriculture and allied activities and non-farm sector activities.

As envisaged the model scheme, all commercial banks have issued instructions for inclusion of short-term fund requirement for meeting the needs of allied activities like dairy, poultry of farm machinery as also the working capital requirement for non-farm activities biding undertaken by farmers in arriving at limit. However, the instructions issued by the various banks have been at variance.

1. Some of the banks have restricted such additional credit @ 10 per cent to 30 per cent of the crop limit sanctioned.
2. Few banks have instructed their branches to sanction a fixed amount per activity to meet the working capital requirement. Others have issued instructions

indicating that these requirements should be reckoned as a part of the overall limit sanctioned for crop and no separate limit need be worked out for the purpose.

3. A few other banks have advised their branches to calculated the actual requirement subject to some ceilings.
4. Some other banks have clubbed attired activities and non-farm sector for arriving at the limits together while a few. have advised their branches to work their requirement separately.
5. Requirement for consumption purposes, have been included as a part of either allied and/or non farm sector requirement.
6. One of the banks has linked consumption credit to compulsory saving by stipulating a minimum saving of 10% of the limit sanctioned for crop subject to maximum of Rs. 50,000 there by implying that if certain borrowers do not want consumption credit, they were exempted from compulsory saving.

The syndicate bank has fixed such additional credit at Rs. 1500 for one activity subject to maximum of Rs. 3000 whereas the Canara Bank put the additional credit limit at 20% of limit for agriculture and allied activities.

Margin and Security Norms

All the banks have issued in their respective circulars on Kisan Credit Card about margin and security norms. While majority of the banks have specifically mentioned margin requirement for different slabs of sanctioned amount, others have advised that the cards would be covered by norms as applicable in the case of other agriculture advances.

Facilities of Drawal at Other Branches

One of the ideas behind Kisan Credit Card was to allow flexibility to the former for drawal of cash at various branches of the issuing bank particularly those located in semi-urban areas to facilitate easy availability of cash for purchase of agri-inputs like fertilizers and pesticides. Though most of the banks had allowed this facility to the cardholder some have restricted this facility to the identified branches within the district only. However, wherever this facility has been extended, it has been allowed for only literate cardholders. Cardholders who are illiterate will have to operate on the limit from the issuing branch only. The banks which have allowed this facility to their cardholders had advised their branches to charge a specific amount as service charges of the cardholder withdraws cash at a branch(s) other than the issuing branch. The amount of such service charge/ commission ranged from 2% to 3% of the cash withdraw it is felt that the per centage is quite high and rather than being a facility, it appeared to work as deterrent. In our cases, both syndicate bank and Canara Banks have not provided such facility of drawal at other branches to the KCC holders.

Repayment Instruction

Although the limit sanctioned under the Kisan Credit Card is in the nature of revolving cash credit and each drawal is repayable within 12 months, yet all the banks have advised their branches to fix specific repayment norms while sanctioning credit limit under Kisan Credit Cards. All the banks have followed by procedure of fixing sub-limit under the Kisan Card and operations on the next sub limit are permitted only when the repayment of the previous sub-limits are made. This means that if a carnet has been sanctioned a limit with sub-limits for khariff and rabi crops, he would be allowed to draw khariff limit only when full/ partial amount under khariff limit has been repaid. Similarly, to draw upon the rabi limit, specific portion of outstanding under khariff sub-limit will have to be repaid. In our case, the syndicate bank has not issued any specific instructions regarding repayment of loan. But the Canara Bank has specified that loan should be repaid immediately after harvesting of crops and within the period of one year. If the loan has been taken for the long-term crops like sugarcane, banana etc., it should be repaid immediately after harvesting.

Insurance of the Cardholder

Although in the model scheme circulated by RBI/NABARD insurance of the cardholder by the issuing banks was not recommended, some of the commercial banks have introduced the provision of insurance to the cardholder in the scheme implemented by them. Both syndicate bank and Canara bank have introduced the scheme of personal accident insurance to the cardholders. In our field study it is found that, the cardholders of syndicate bank are covered under personal accident insurance scheme and are paying a premium of Rs. 5 per annum. Canara bank provides personal accident insurance upto Rs. 50,000 to all farmers below the age of 70 years who availed crop loan under the KCC scheme.

Introduction of insurance is good features introduced by some commercial banks with a view to not only add to the marketing component of the Kisan Card product but also the bank for the amount borrowed under the card. With effect from the year 2001-02. Union Finance Minister has proposed to make the insurance compulsory for all Kisan Cardholders and the premium would be shared by the card issuing institutions.

Issue of Cheque Book

One of the basic ideas behind introducing Kisan Credit Card was to provide-flexibility and convenience to the farmer in borrowing and repayment of money. In order to facilitate the drawal of cash both at the issuing as well as other designated branches some of the banks have issued Cheque Book to the cardholders. This facility, however, has been restricted to only literate borrowers. In certain other banks, this facility has been given only to farmers holding good record. In the remaining banks, the drawls of cash are allowed only through the debit slip of the card issuing branch only.

Service Charges

For issuing Kisan Credit Card, most of the banks have been levying fees under different names such as service charges, follow up chares, out of pocket expenses, inspection charges etc., to cover their cost. In some of the banks, these charges are quite substantial. Some of the banks have also been charging inspection charges as well as application processing charges from the borrower. For replacement of lost card or damaged card a few of the banks have been charging as high as Rs. 200 from the borrower to provide duplicate card. Similarly, one or two banks have also been levying charges as much as Rs. 200. As penalty in case of not linking of card. In our study it is found that no one has paid any charge or fees to banks toward obtaining Kisan Credit Card.

Opening of Saving Bank Account

Except Syndicate Bank, none of the other commercial banks have made it compulsory for borrower to open a saving bank account with the bank branch in order to avail the facility of Kisan Credit Card.

Payment of Interest on Credit Balance in the Saving Bank Account

Except a few, most of the banks have not given specific guidelines to their branches in the Kisan Credit Card account. A few banks who have issued instructions in this regard are either prescribing certain minimum credit balance for a specific period or paying interest @ 4 per cent on minimum balance from the 10th to the last day of the month. In absence of this facility many farmers may not be induced to maintain credit balance in the Kisan Credit Card account and this could affect the recovery of dues.

Crop Insurance

Among the public sector banks, have provided guidelines

to their branch managers in the circular relating to Kisan Card on coverage of crop insurance under Rastriya Krishi Bima Yojna. For instance, Syndicate Bank have advised its branches that premium for crop insurance to be worked out on the basis of limit sanctioned for crop insurance. Other banks have advised their branch managers to debit the crop insurance premium to the borrowers account wherever insurance scheme is available.

Summary

Agricultural growth is crucial for alleviating rural poverty. Access to institutional credit to more farmers and appropriate quantity and quality of agricultural credit are crucial for realising the full potential of agriculture as a profitable activity. Recognizing the crucial role of credit, the Tenth Five-Year Plan (2002-07) envisages a substantial jump in credit flows to agriculture to Rs. 7,36,750 crore in the plan period as compared to the credit flow of Rs. 2,29,956 crore achieved in the Ninth Five-Year Plan period. Credit flow to agriculture sector from all formal sources amounted to Rs. 70,810 crore in 2002-03 and Rs. 86,981 crore in 2003-04, much below the levels envisaged in the Tenth Plan. Concerned over the slower growth of agriculture credit, the Government announced a comprehensive policy on June 18, 2004. The policy envisages a 30 per cent increase in credit to agriculture sector in 2004-05 over an estimated credit flow of Rs. 80,000 crore in 2003-04. The implementation of the policy has been entrusted to PSBs, private sector banks, regional rural banks (RRBs) and cooperative banks. The policy has indicated that each rural and semi-urban branch of commercial banks, on an average, will take up at least two to three new investment projects in the area of plantation and horticulture, fisheries, organic farming, agro-processing, livestock, micro-irrigation, sprinkler irrigation, watershed management, village pond development and other agricultural activities. NABARD has been asked to advise District-Level Technical Committees to review the scales of finance to meet the realistic credit needs of farmers, especially for capital intensive agricultural operations. The Budget for 2004-05, presented in the Parliament on July 8, 2004, proposed doubling of credit to agriculture in three years and announced further measures to achieve the target growth in agricultural credit. These measures include holding the sponsor bank of each RRB squarely responsible for the performance of RRB under its control and an incentive scheme under which RRBs adopting new governance standards and abiding by prudential regulations will qualify for receiving funds from the Government for their restructuring. And the Kisan Credit Card scheme which enables the farmers to obtain loans for their agricultural operations on a revolving cash credit limit basis has been introduced by all the banks with effect from Khariff 1999 season. The Kisan Credit Card scheme basically aims at providing adequate and timely credit support to the farmers for agricultural operations including purchase of inputs.

5

Regional Rural Banks and Agricultural Development in Mysore District: Case Study Analysis

This chapter mainly focuses on the Mysore District economy, in terms of geographical background, occupational structure, industrial development, agricultural scenario and banking progress in the district. The primary focus of the present chapter is on ascertaining and discussing the factors responsible for the success or weakness of the regional rural banking programmes and to assess their impact up on the farming community. A detailed case study analysis has been presented in this chapter.

Profile of Study Area

Mysore district is one of the important districts of Karnataka State for several reasons. Mysore is the name by which Karnataka State was known prior to 1973. Karnataka State was the name "Mysore". Mysore city is the headquarters of the district and also a revenue division.

Mysore district is known as the "garden city" of India,

on account of its proximity to the famous Brindavan Gardens that are laid out at the Krishnaraja Sagar, a reservoir across the Cauvery. The districts (city) is also known throughout the world for the pomp and gaiety with which the traditional "Dasara" festival is held here annually during the Navaratri (September–October). The tourists throng from all over the country and abroad in great numbers to witness "Jamboo Savari" the chief attraction of occasion.

In Mysore District there are seven taluks 33 hoblis and 1257 in habited villages in the district. The total area of the district is 6269 sq. km.

Location and Size

Mysore district is situated in the Southern part of Karnataka State. The district lies between 11°60 and 20° 17- north latitude and 75° 18 and 77 ° 77 east longitude. Hassan Mandya, and Bangalore Districts bound it on the North; on the South by Cannonore District of Kerala States and Chamarajanagar district of Karnataka State, West by Kodagu district of Karnataka.

Table 5.1
Administrative Divisions of Mysore District

Sl. No.	*Sub-Divisions and Taluks*	*No. of Hoblies*	*No. of Villages*	*No. of Towns*	*Area in sq. km*
1.	Mysore Sub - division				
	(a) Mysore	4	136	0	815
	(b) Nanjangud	5	178	0	982
	(c) T. Narasipura	5	128	2	599
2.	Hunsur Sub-division				
	(a) Hunsur	4	192	0	897
	(b) K.R. Nagar	6	150	0	605
	(c) Periyapatna	4	199	1	815
	H.D. Kote	5	274	3	1618
	Total	**33**	**1257**	**6**	**6269**

Source: District Statistical Office, Mysore.

Climate and Rainfall

The climate of Mysore district is similar to that of neighbouring districts of Mandya and Bangalore. The period from March to May is one of continuous increase in temperature. April is usually the hottest month with a mean daily maximum temperature of about 74°C and the mean daily minimum temperature of about 21°C on some days. The day temperature in the hot season of may go about 36°C.

The district is exposed to both the monsoons but receives the major part of its rainfall from the south west monsoon. This monsoon usually sets in about the end of May or early in June and it continuous with some intervals till the end of September. The north east monsoon commences in October and ends usually by the end of December. Then the cold weather periods follows and lasts till the end of February. The hot weather period begins with March and increases its intensity towards the end of May. However, there is occasional relief from pre-monsoon thunder storms. There is not a month without some amount of rainfull and that the normal for all months is considerable except for the cold months of December to March in the district. The highest normal rainfall occurs variably in the month of October in the North-East monsoon, for all taluks with the second highest in both May and September.

Soil

Klages in 1958 has quoted "Every nation is a bit of soil and humanity." Therefore no student of civilization forgets for an instant the fundamental importance of soil. Practically it is the source of all man's food. So much so, that man gets nearly all of his food from the soil.

There is no resource more significant than soil to Mysore District is complex reflecting a variety of parent materials variations in the intensity of irrigation and land use and hydrological hazards. According to ordinary usage. The soil capability is understood as the ability to raise crops depending upon the physical–chemical–biological combination of a soil. Clay soils may frequently have only a low actual productivity due to water shortage and the difficulty of cultivation. At the same time their large nutrient reserves may give them a high potential productivity which can only be exploited by means of suitable farming methods – a common feature in the flood plains of the study area.

The distribution of soils strongly affects the pattern of Mysore districts land use intensity and agricultural land – use occupancy owing to limited progress made in biological and mechanical farm production techniques, specially the restricted use of chemical fertilizers and hybridized seeds. However, where higher level of agricultural technology has been achieved with intensification and mechanization. The modification of the inherent soil characteristics has been accompanied by a domination of soil fertility.

The study area is predominantly covered by red loamy and red soils which are derived from granites and geniuses. They vary from pure sandy soils to typical black cotton soils. The western taluks of Periyapatna, Hunsur, H. D. Kote and parts of Krishnarajnagar and covered with lilly terrain. In the east parts of T. Narasipura and Nanjangud taluks are also covered with hilly terrain and contain red shallow gravelly soils. The taluks contain deep red loamy soils occasionally interrupted with black soils. The red soils are generally shallow to deep. Their colour is red to pale brown and well drained.

Agricultural Development

Agricultural development is a special field which is influenced by natural environment upon nature and its distribution of man's activities and qualities. In the development of agriculture water, climate and natural resources play a predominant role.

Mysore district is predominantly agricultural. It appears from a perusal of the census reports. That the livelihood pattern in the district has more or less been constant for the last 60 years. The agricultural practice however under went considerable change since 1972, for until then, the district was an arid travel of land with a backward economy, with additional and by to days. Standard's out moded agricultural practices. The district was often faced with droughts and famines.

Agriculture in Mysore is characterized by small holdings. A majority of the farmers has landholdings of one hectare and constituted about 63.10 per cent. According to 2000–2001 agricultural census. There are 3.70 hector of land holders. 3.80 lakh hector, of land was use for agriculture . (But the average land grant is 1.02 hector). The total land cultivated very tiny landholders constituted 27.11%. The small land-holders constitute 72.59 per cent in between the about 2 land holder constitute 24.38% middle land owners constitute 12.68% and finally the big land owners constituted 3.24% of the total land grants, sugar cane, cotton and become an important commercial crop in the district following the extension of irrigation facilities.

Economic Activities

1. *Industries*

   The industries are the major components that form the economic bar of Mysore district. There are several types of industries such as Silk Industry Sandal Oil Industry, Scented Sticks, Electric Products, Sugar Industry, Beedi, Motor Cycle Industries, Mysore Fertilizer and Chemical Factory, Textile Industry and manufacture of tyres, which contribute greatly to the economy of the district.

2. *Tourism*

   Tourism is another major component that forms the economic base of the district being a place of historical importance, attracts a large tourist population. A number of tourist area cover the Chamundi Hills, the

Table 5.2
Mysore District Population According to 2001 Census

Sl. No.	District	Total	Taluk 2001 Census		Rural		Urban	
			Males	Females	Males	Females	Males	Females
1.	H.D. Kote	242615	123042	119573	116853	113719	6189	5854
2.	Hunsur	258138	130049	128089	107654	106591	22395	21498
3.	K.R. Nagar	239155	120515	118640	104926	103626	15589	15014
4.	Nanjangud	358415	182729	175686	158345	151850	24384	23836
5.	Mysore	1024410	521624	502786	121720	116890	399904	385896
6.	Periyapatna	224022	115813	108209	108212	100888	7601	7321
7.	T. Narasipura	26,24,911	1335841	1289070	843013	813297	492828	475773
	Total	**26,24,911**	**1335841**	**1289070**	**843013**	**813297**	**492828**	**475773**

Source : District Statistical Office , Mysore.

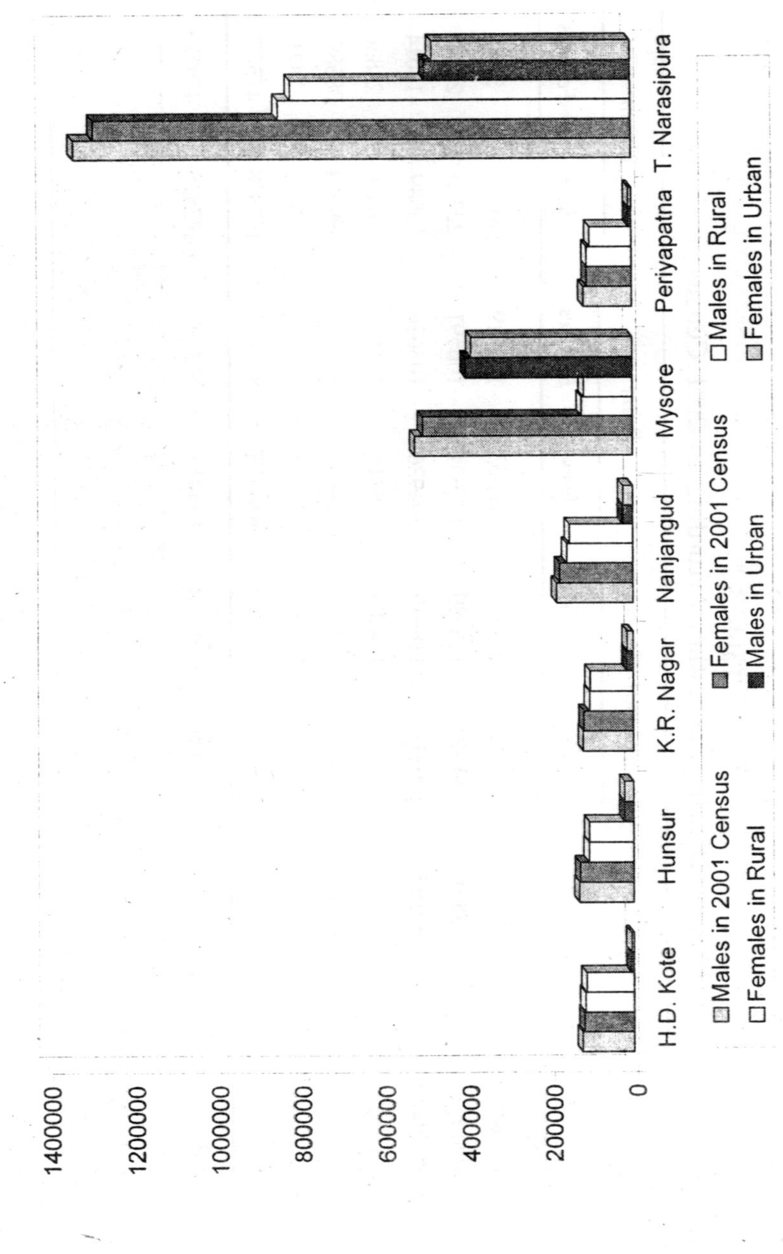
1400000
1200000
1000000
800000
600000
400000
200000
0
H.D. Kote
Hunsur
K.R. Nagar
Nanjangud
Mysore
Periyapatna
T. Narasipura
Males in 2001 Census
Females in 2001 Census
Males in Rural
Females in Rural
Males in Urban
Females in Urban

bird century, the brindavan gardens, temples, and old attract buildings, etc. Which attract more than a million tourists in a year.

3. *Commercial Activities*

   The old city is predominantly the business district. This area is concentrated with retail and wholesale traders, offices, hosiery industries and commercial entertainments. These activities are spread along the taluk of Mysore, Nanjangud, Hunsur in other area of concentration of commercial activity to all taluks.

Population of the District

In Mysore District the total population has increased to 26,24,911 during 2001 census. The details of population according to 2001 census in Mysore district are presented in Table 5.2.

Occupational Structure

The occupational distribution of the rural population of Mysore district throws light on the social and economic conditions in different taluks. By and large it speaks about the state of the agricultural economy in the district. Economic development, since the introduction of irrigation facilities created by the KRS dam across the river Cauvery in the district has brought about changes in the occupational distribution.

Out of the total population of about 26,24,911 crores in the district the work force 10,22,912, crores constituting 37.29 per cent of the distribution of working force as per 1991and 2000 census is 4.2 and 4.4 respectively.

Nearly 65 per cent of the working population is engaged in agriculture workers engaged in manufacturing and household activities consist only 8 per cent of the working population. Agriculture is the main stay for bulk of the population, which indicates the industrial backwardness of the district.

Irrigation Facilities

About 24 per cent of the area sown in the district has irrigation facilities. Two taluks viz. K.R. Nagar and T. Narasipur account for nearly 70 per cent of the net area sown. Main sources of irrigation are wells and canals.

Cauvery is the main river of the district with its tributaries Kabini Lakshmanathirtha and Suvarnavathi.

Table 5.3
The Area Under Cultivation of Important Food and Commercial Crops

Important crops	*Area under cultivation (in Hectors)*	*Production in Tones*
Rice	72,321	2,76,963
Ragi	1,12,235	1,09,272
Jowar	92,559	1,78,897
Maize	10,477	31,431
Minor millets	5,481	8,221
Grams	2,306	1,195
Other pulses	68,391	34,195
Tur	7,838	3,914
Sugarcane	26,341	16,31,100
Groundnut	19,703	1,97,030
Cotton	1,534	767
Mulberry	1,04,295	0
Tobacco	15,800	11,116

Source: District Horticulture Department, Mysore.

Only 28 per cent of the net area sown is used for raising multiple crops. There is a very good scope for encouraging intensive use of the land resources and also extending cultivable area.

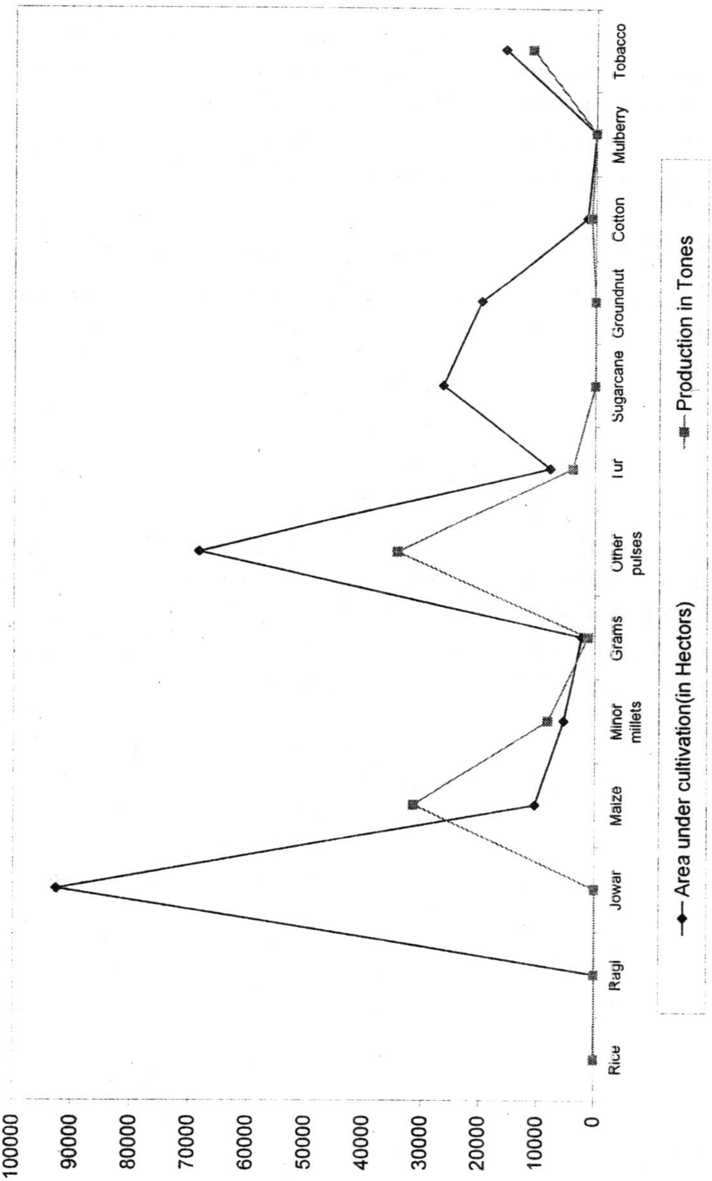
100000
90000
80000
70000
60000
50000
40000
30000
20000
10000
0
Rice
Ragi
Jowar
Maize
Minor millets
Grams
Other pulses
Tur
Sugarcane
Groundnut
Cotton
Mulberry
Tobacco
Area under cultivation(in Hectors)
Production in Tones

The Kabini project is one of the major irrigation projects. Other irrigation projects, which will benefit the district, are Harangi Reservoir Project located in Coorg district and Hemavathi project located in Hassan district.

The ground water survey indicates that there is good potential to increase irrigation facilities through sinking wells.

Horticulture

Though various types of fruits are growths in the district. The entire quantity of fruits is consumed within the district itself, except for bananas, which are sent to Bangalore, and other neighbouring districts.

Forests

Mysore is the richest district in the state as far as the forest resources are concerned. The district has an area of lakh hectares unbar forest i.e. about 27per cent of the geographical area is covered by forest.

Table 5.4 gives information about the area covered by forests in the 7 taluks of Mysore district.

Table 5.4
Area Covered by Forest in the District

Taluks	*Forest Area (Hectares)*
1. H.D.Kote	28,475
2. Hunsur	7,786
3. K.R. Nagar	1,66
4. Mysore	3,216
5. Nanjangud	3,690
6. Periyapatna	14,816
7. T. Narasipur	184

Source: Dept. of Forest, Mysore District, Mysore.

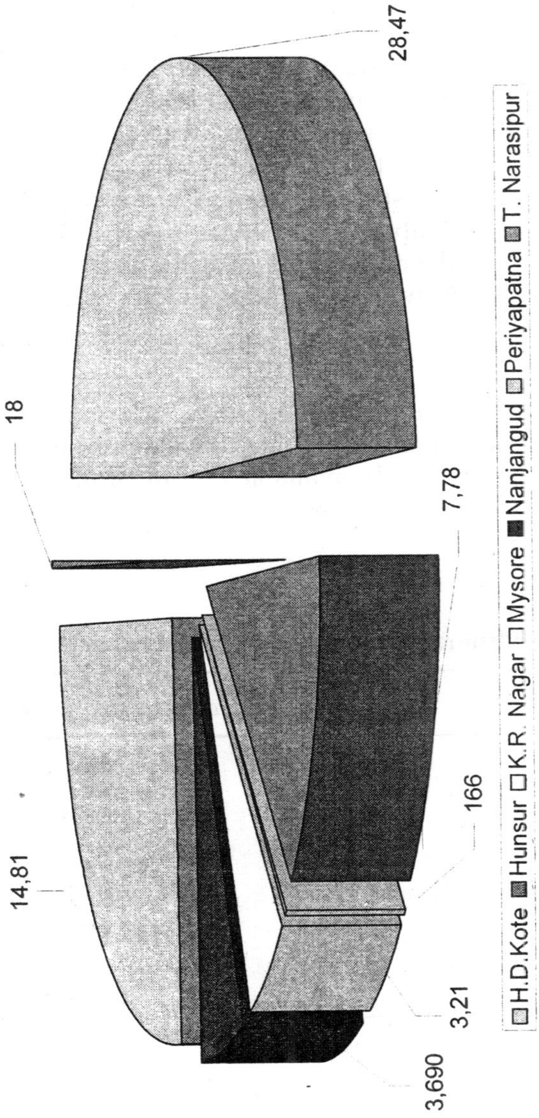

28,47
18
7,78
166
14,81
3,21
3,690
H.D.Kote Hunsur K.R. Nagar Mysore Nanjangud Periyapatna T. Narasipur

Sericulture

Mysore District accounts nearly 50 per cent of the total production of silk in the state. Sericulture industry is one of the major cottage industries in this district. Out of total 2.35 lakhs acres under mulberry plantation in the state. The district accounts for nearly 1.04 lakh acres. The Industry is concentrated mostly in the taluks of Nanjangud, T.Narasipur, and H.D.Kote. The estimated annual production of silk in the district is worth about Rs. 12 crore. Nearly 1 lakh persons are engaged in mulberry cultivation, seed rearing, silk reeling, twisting and cloth weaving in the district.

Minerals

The district is not endowed with rich mineral wealth minerals like magnite, soap stone, limestone, Chromite and graphite are reported to be available in comparatively, smaller, quantities. The estimated reserve of mineral resources is given the Table 5.5.

Table 5.5
Mineral Resources in the District

Mineral	*Estimated Deposits (Million Tones)*
1. Iron ore	13.20
2. Magnate	2.00
3. Chromate	0.03
4. Cyanide and Sillinenite	0.02
5. Graphite	0.03
6. Lime stone	0.05

Source: Forest Department, Mysore Dist.

The iron, chromites are deposits and graphite resources available in the district are found to be of low grade not considered feasible at present for commercial exploitation.

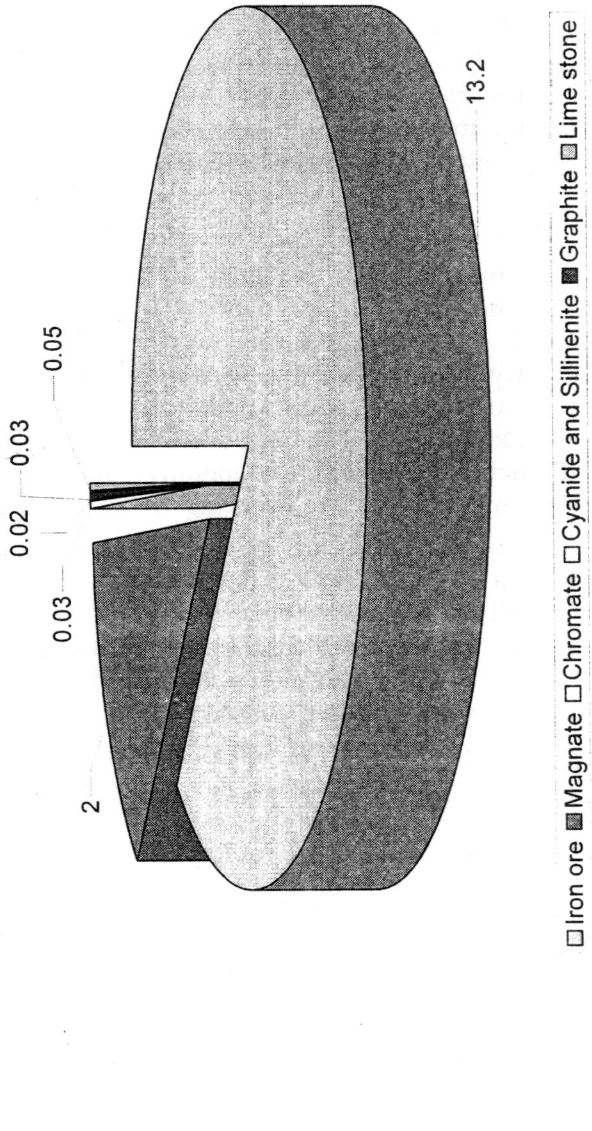
13.2
0.05
0.03
0.02
0.03
2
Iron ore
Magnate
Chromate
Cyanide and Sillinenite
Graphite
Lime stone

The Magnate is found at Hullahalli and Karya village in Nanjangud taluk and at Mavinahalli and Tayur in Mysore taluk.

Infrastructure Facilities in Mysore District

Infrastructure facilities such as roads transport facilities and vehicles, railways, communication, power, water supply; credit facilities, etc., are absolutely necessary for attracting and prompting industries in an area. In this background let us see the position of these facilities in Mysore district.

Financial Institutions

Banking and financial facilities are considered to be adequate in the district as it enjoy the services of a wide net work of commercial banks, agriculture and rural development banks, cooperative banks etc. There are (227) branches of commercial banks spread all over the district. The State Bank of Mysore has been designated as a lead bank for the district. Twenty-seven cooperative and 20 primary land development banks are working in the district.

A branch of the Karnataka Industrial Co-operative Bank is working in Mysore having a district Jurisdiction for financing small-scale units. A regional office of the Karnataka State Financial Corporation (KSFC) also is working in Mysore City with Jurisdiction over Mysore, Mandya, Dakshina Kannada, Coorg and Hassan districts.

Mysore is the second largest industrial district of the state of Karnataka. State Bank of Mysore, having the largest number of branches in the district is the lead bank of this district. The bank also its zonal office in Mysore city guiding all its branches in Mysore and in the contiguous eight districts. Further, a specialized Small-Scale Industry branch (SSI Branch-first of its kind in the bank) was also opened in Mysore city in the year 1993, to improve the bank's coverage of industries in this area.

The government is indicating to promote Mysore district as the alternate industrial hub to Bangalore and their Department of Industries and Commerce has already recommended acquisition of additional land of around 3,900 acres for industrial purposes in the district. Accordingly, the targeted outlay of funds under the credit plan for every year is around Rs. 34.03 crore. In spite of all these efforts, the industrial growth in the district has been sluggish. Further, the growth of industrial advances of the bank, in this region has not been proportionate even to the level of industrial development.

Cauvery Grameena Bank and Rural Development in Mysore District

Cauvery Grameena Bank was established on the 2nd October, 1976. In the beginning the bank confined its operations to Hassan district from December 1980 with the bifurcation of Mysore district into Mysore and Chamarajanagar districts during 1997-98 the bank is now operating in three districts viz., Mysore, Chamarajanagar and Hassan.

Cauvery Grameena Bank plays an important role in meeting the financial requirements in rural areas. It is important to note that the financial support to the marginal farmers, landless – labourers and rural artisans is provided through the Cauvery Grameena Bank.

Business Philosophy of the Bank

The bank which was established with the objective of ameliorating the economic conditions by granting loans to small and marginal farmers, agricultural labourers, artisans small entrepreneurs and persons of small means engaged in trade or other productive activities has been implementing Government sponsored poverty alleviation programmes, like IRDP, for the economic upliftment of the weaker sections of the society and also concentrating on priority sector lending to the target group in line with the underlying business philosophy.

Branch Network of Cauvery Grameena Bank

The district-wise distribution of branch network of Cauvery Grameena Bank is presented in the Table 5.6.

Table 5.6
No. of Branches of Cauvery Grameena Bank

District	*Rural*	*Semi-urban*	*Urban*	*Total*
Mysore	44	5	6	55
Chamarajnagar	20	4	-	24
Hassan	38	6	-	44
Total	**102**	**15**	6	**123**

Source: Cauvery Grameena Bank Annual Reports.

During the year 2003-04 one new city branch namely Thonachi Koppal Layout in Mysore was opened. The Devanur branch in Nanjangud Taluk Mysore district was relocated to Aloganchi Village.

Cauvery Grameena Bank has 123 branches over the three districts, out of which 102 branches are located in rural areas. The take care of the credit needs of the rural poor in these respective service areas, which totally amounts to 1423 services area villages.

Share Capital of the Bank

During the year 2003-04 in terms of Section 6 of Regional Rural Banks Act 1976 the Government of India. The Government of Karnataka and the sponsor bank i.e. State Bank of Mysore have subscribed to the banks share capital in the ratio 50 : 15 : 35 respectively. During the year there is no change in the issued and paid-up capital of the bank which stood at Rs.10,000 thousands the revamping fund to

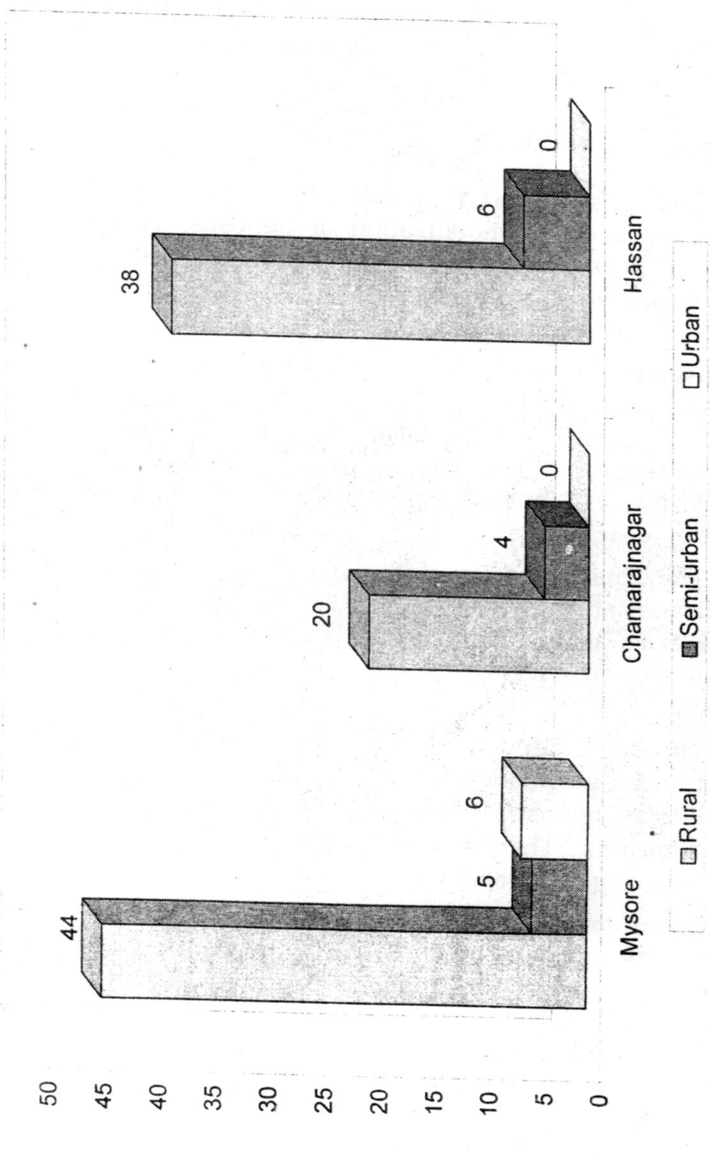
50
45
40
35
30
25
20
15
10
5
0
44
5
6
20
4
0
38
6
0
Mysore
Chamarajnagar
Hassan
Rural
Semi-urban
Urban

the extent of Rs.1,32,873 thousands contributed by the Government of India. Government of Karnataka and sponsor bank is shown as share capital restructuring fund pending receipt of the Government of India approval to increase the authorized and issued capital of the bank.

Deposit Mobilization

The most important source of the banks for enlarging their resources is mobilization of deposits. Thus deposits have a greater significance for the RRBs and in turn for the development of rural economy.

The total deposit of the banks grew by Rs. 2,37,740 thousands which represents nearly 100% growth compared to last year and stood at Rs. 1,47,565 thousands as at the end of March 2001–02 as against Rs. 12,38,225 thousands as at the end of previous year. The growth represents a rise of 19.20% (11.38% in the previous year) in the deposit level during year.

The total deposits of the bank grew by Rs. 2,58,841 thousands and stood at Rs. 20,26,387 thousands as at the year 2004-05 as against Rs. 17,67,546 thousands as at the end of previous year. The growth represents 14.64% in deposit level during the year.

The total deposit of the bank grew by Rs. 3,10,329 thousands and stood at Rs. 23,36,626 thousands as at the year 2005-06 as against Rs. 20,26,387 thousands as at the end of previous year. The growth represents 15.3% in the deposit level during the year.

The total deposits of the Bank grew by Rs. 36,95,81 thousands and stood at Rs. 27,05,207 thousands as at the year 2007-08 as against Rs. 23,36,626 thousand as at the end of previous year. The growth represents 15.80% in the deposits level during the year.

Table 5.7
Deposits Mobilization of Cauvery Grameena Bank in Mysore District

District	2001-02		2003-04		2004-05		2005-06		2007-08	
	Amount	%	*Amount*	%	*Amount*	%	*Amount*	%	*Amount*	%
Mysore	710650	48%	888409	50%	980229	48%	1133019	48%	1377971	51%
Chamarajanagar	276777	19%	324038	18%	390239	19%	465924	20%	516319	19%
Hassan	488538	33%	555099	32%	65519	33%	737683	32%	811917	30%
Total	147565	100%	1767546	100%	2026387	100%	2336626	100	2705207	100%

Source : Cauvery Grameena Bank, Annual Reports.

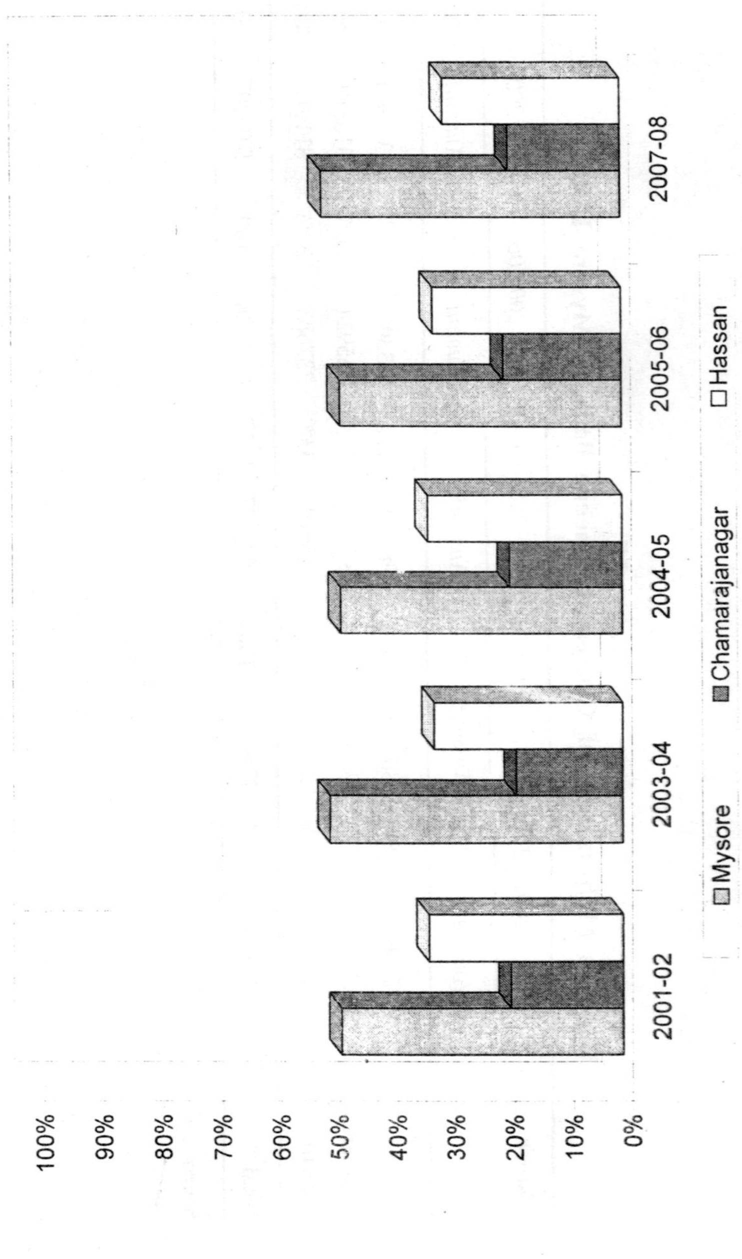
100%
90%
80%
70%
60%
50%
40%
30%
20%
10%
0%
2001-02
2003-04
2004-05
2005-06
2007-08
Mysore
Chamarajanagar
Hassan

Demand Deposits and Term Deposits

The level of demand deposits and time deposits and this proportion to the Banks total are as follows. After deregulation of interest rates on deposits. The bank is periodically reviewing the interest rate payable on the deposits based on the market trend and the credit policy announced by Reserve Bank of India from time accordingly, the interest rates on term deposits were reviewed and revised 2 times during the year and were last remained with effect from 1st Oct. 2003 and they range from 4.00% (for deposits of 15 days to 45 days) to 6.25% (for deposits of 3 years and above) earlier to this the rates varied from 4.25% to 6.25% consequent to these changes the cost of deposits has come down to 7.70% from 9.12% 2002 per branch deposit of the Bank has increased from Rs.19,153 thousands as at the end of March 2007 to Rs. 22,001 thousands as at the end of March 2008. Correspondingly per employee deposit has also increased from Rs. 4417 thousands to Rs. 5068 thousands.

Borrowings of Cauvery Grameena Bank

The ratio of borrowings to total advances stood at 30.41% as against 35.27% at the end of the 2005-06. The sponsor bank confines its refinance only to SAO, OSAO, and MT (non-schematic). Its refinance terms were on par with NABARD all along after RBI permitted commercial banks to determine independently. The rate at which refinance is given to the RRBs sponsored by them it had increased its refinance rates as under with effect from 1999-2000. Due to the above changes the average cost of borrowings has increased to 8.18% from 7.07% in the previous year. The Bank continues to be prompt in repayment of dues to NABARD and sponsor bank, 2001-02. The ratio of borrowings to total advances stood at 20.06% as against 28.23% as at the end of previous year.

The average cost of borrowings has decreased to 8.18% from 8.40% in the previous year. The bank continues to be promoting in repayment of dues to NABARD and sponsor

Bank and there are no defaults. 2002-03 the ratio of borrowings to total advances stood at 6.49% as against 20.06% as at the end of previous year.

The average cost of borrowings has decreased to 6.74% from 8.18% in the previous year. This reduction in cost was possible by judicious decision in reduction and also repayment of borrowings during the surplus season. The bank continues to be prompt in repayment of dues to NABARD and sponsor bank and there are no defaults. 2005-06 the year ratio of borrowings to total advances stood at 7.86% as against 6.49% as at the end of year.

The average cost of borrowings has decreased to 7.14% from 8.02%. This reduction in cost was possible by judicious availment of refinance and also repayment of borrowing during the surplus season. The bank continues to be prompt in repayment of dues to NABARD and sponsor bank and there are no defaults during the year.

The Role of Cauvery Grameena Bank in Agricultural Development

Cauvery Grameena Bank is directly and indirectly supporting agriculture development in numerous ways. Cauvery Grameena Bank give agriculture term loans for land based activities such as minor irrigation drip irrigation, to punches tractors/tillers to undertake/develop sericulture and other such productivity by using modern skills and technology, so that there will be agriculture development.

Cauvery Grameena Bank also helps agriculture development by giving crop loans for meeting part costs of cultivation of crops repayable after the crops are raised and marketed.

Crop loans are advanced with the object of providing financial assistance to small and marginal farmers to purchase seeds. Chemical fertilizers and manure, pesticides, diesel and oil, to hire tractors, threshers and to pay wage to the labourers.

This is production oriented loan and helps in raising the crop and thereby development of agriculture.

Cauvery Grameena Bank also contributes to agriculture development by giving loans to allied activities such as for purchase of bullocks and others.

Now let us discuss in detail the Cauvery Grameena Bank advances to the development of agriculture in Mysore district.

The bank has taken up promoting self-help groups during the year with the financial assistance of Rs. 4.30 lakh from NABARD as SHPI for promoting and linkage of 300 SHGs through 20 selected branches. The bank has formed/promoted 374 groups and credit linked 280 groups with an amount of Rs. 1.05 crores under the project.

The bank has established a "Women Development Cell" at Head Office, with the assistance of NABARD in 1996. The Cell has been making efforts to provide increased thrust to enhance lending to women beneficiaries through the process of gender sensitization programmes, establishing linkage with voluntary agencies working in the area etc. Consequently, there has been a steady increase in the lending's to women beneficiaries, as evident from the data furnished in the Table-5.8.

Table 5.8
Credit Assistance to Women Beneficiaries

Sl. No	*Year*	*Disbursement*	*Outstanding*	*% to total advance*
1.	2001-02	39032	1975.52	19.19
2.	2004-05	35954	1881.70	16.74
3.	2005-06	99900	2825.00	17.43
4.	2006-07	460500	4318.88	18.77
5.	2007-08	598775	6375.25	20.51

Source: Annual Reports, Cauvery Grameena Bank.

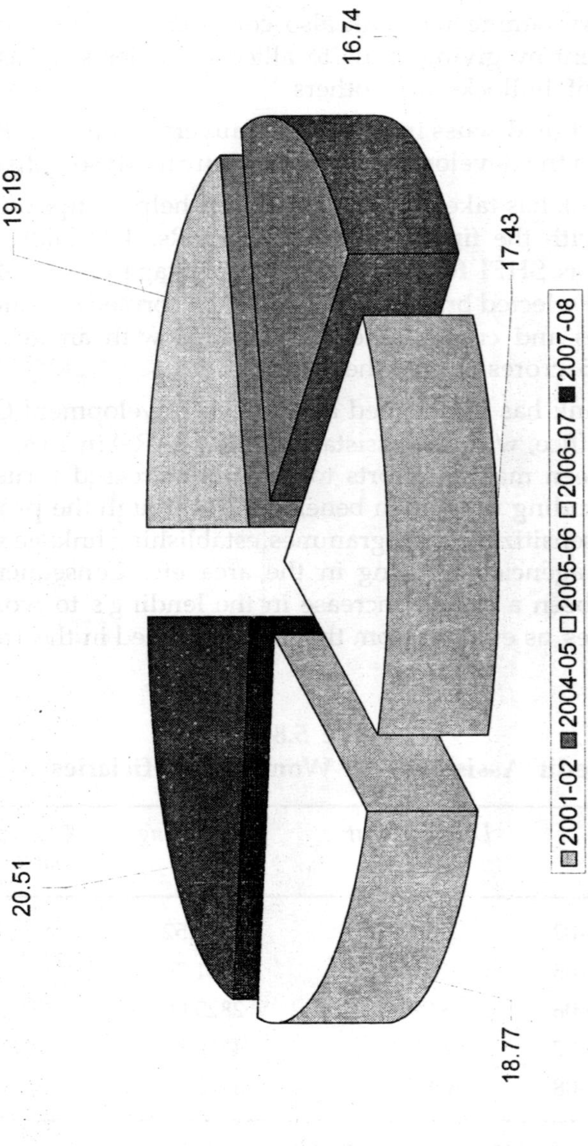
16.74
19.19
17.43
20.51
18.77
2001-02
2004-05
2005-06
2006-07
2007-08

The Women Development Cell conducted Gender Sensitization programme to selected staff of the bank. International Women's Day Celebration was also conducted at Head Office and also at Periyapatna, Nanjangud and T.Narasipura branches. This is need of the hour.

The SHG women members were trained in book-keeping, interest application to the loans, benefits of bank linkage, etc. The women entrepreneurs were assisted by providing marketing facilities free of cost at various local exhibitions, Swadeshi Mela, JSS exhibition cum sale, etc.

Flow of Credit to Agriculture Sector

The bank has implemented the comprehensive packages for farmers as announced by Hon'ble Finance Minister and also initiated necessary action to agriculture sector. The total amount disbursed to agricultural sector is Rs. 132.93 crore against the target of Rs.113.29 crore representing an achievement of 117.33%. The performance during the year 2007-08 is presented in Table 5.9.

Table 5.9
Performance of Bank Credit to Agriculture Sector During 2007-08

(Rs.in lakhs)

Sl. No.	*Particulars*	*Target*	*Achievement*
1.	Crop loans	8761.62	10855.83
2.	Term loans	2567.79	2437.26
	Total	11329.41	13293.09

Source: Annual Reports, Cauvery Grameena Bank.

In order to give more thrust on lending to agriculture and also create awareness among the rural people about the various schemes of the bank "Krishi Utsav" was conducted

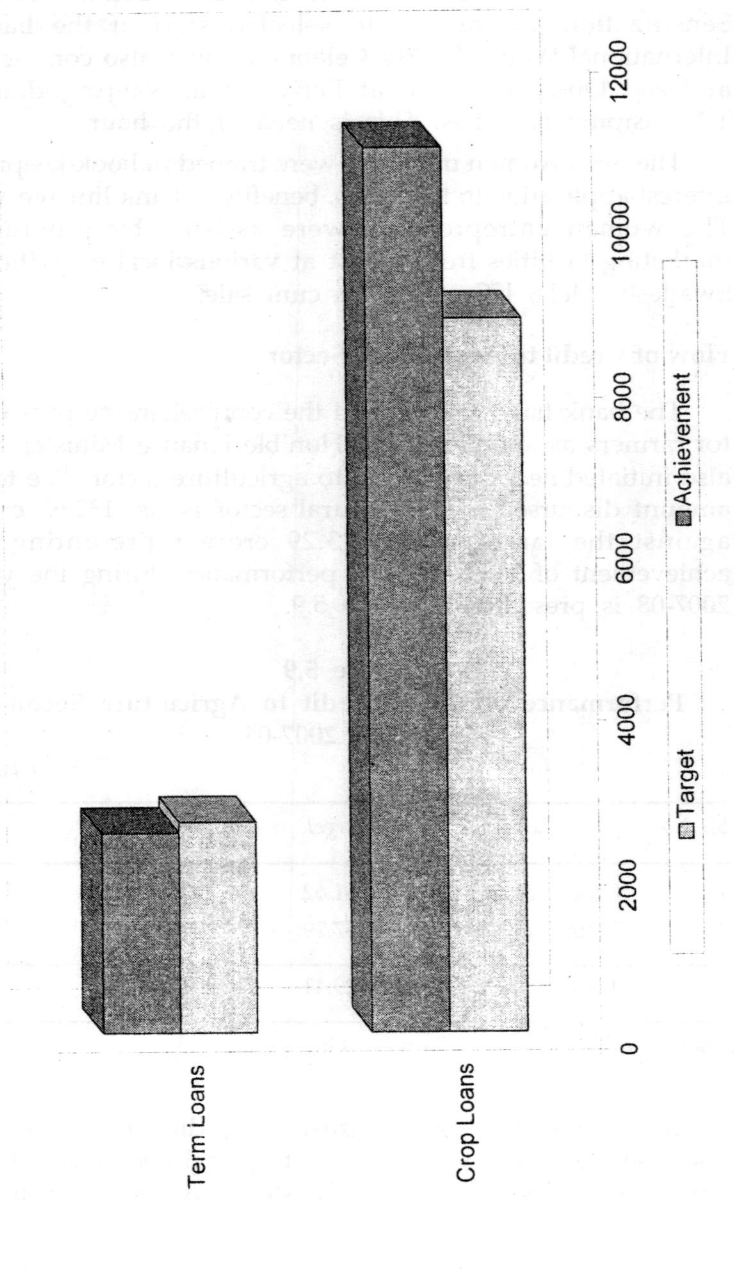
Term Loans
Crop Loans
0
2000
4000
6000
8000
10000
12000
Target
Achievement

at Nanjangud, H.D.Kote and Hunsur centers. A progrmme on pomegranate cultivation was conducted at K.R.Nagar in association with University of Agricultural Sciences and Horticulture Dept., Government of Karnataka. In terms of Government of India guidelines reimbursement of interest at 2% on crop loans amounting to Rs.1,22,63,098 was credit to the borrower's accounts.

Implementation of Government Sponsored Schemes

The bank actively participated in implementing Government Sponsored poverty alleviation programmes. The bank assisted 75 groups under SGSY against a target of 73. Performance of the bank during the year in various government-sponsored programmes is furnished in the Table 5.10. The data in the table clearly shows that there is a favourable trend in all the government schemes.

Table 5.10
Performance – Physical Number of Beneficiaries in Mysore District during 2007-08

Sl. No	*Name of the Scheme*	*Target*	*Achievement*
1.	SGSY – Individual	59	59
2.	SGSY – Group	48	50
3.	SC/ST corporation	54	71
4.	Chaitanya	58	58
5.	Swavalambana	21	33

Source: Annual Reports, Cauvery Grameena Bank.

Farmers Clubs

The bank has actively participated in formation of farmers clubs and has launched 48 new farmers clubs during the year 2007-08. Total number of farmers clubs attached to the branches is 298, with a minimum of one club per rural branch.

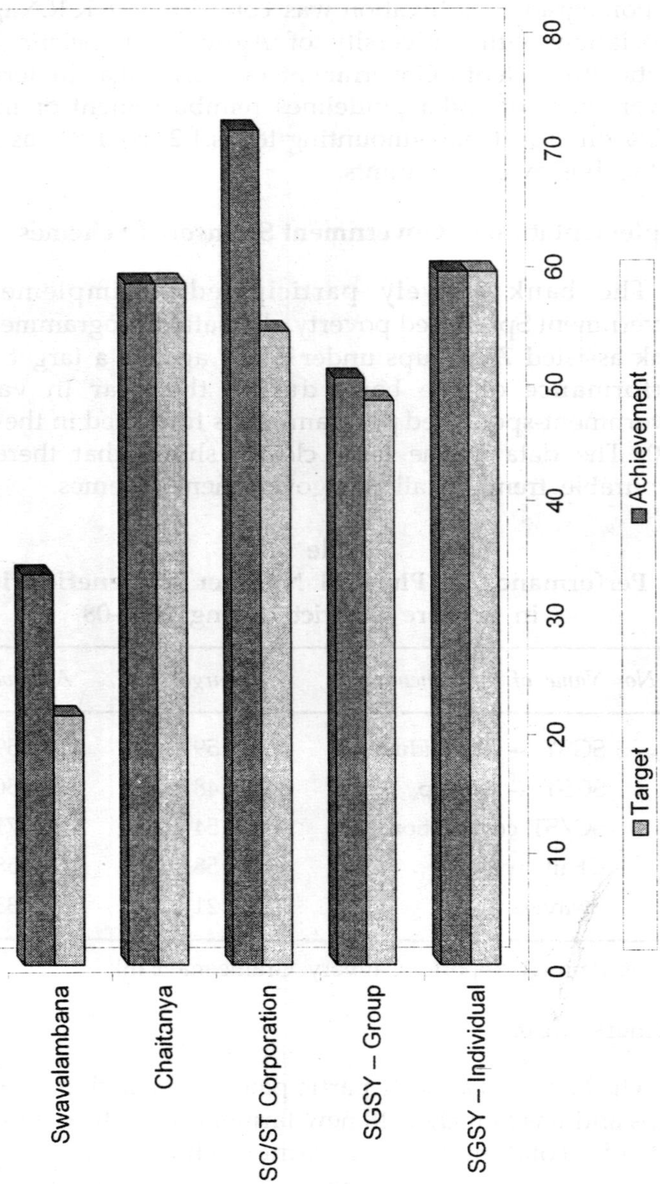
Swavalambana
Chaitanya
SC/ST Corporation
SGSY – Group
SGSY – Individual
0
10
20
30
40
50
60
70
80
Target
Achievement

The Farmers Clubs have also conducted various programmes for the benefit of villagers like animal health check-up, pest control, recovery drives under BOOTS, Self-employment guidance, water management, formation of SHGs, motivation and training camps, sapling distribution and tree planting, etc.

As an innovative measure Vyasaraja Farmers Club attached to T.Narasipura branch is formed exclusively by defaulters. Out of 20 defaulting members, 15 members have cleared the dues and other farmers are also motivated to clear their dues and intend to make its members default free. The branch intends to use this club to have demonstrative effect and form more such clubs to bring defaulters also under financial inclusion. Prerana Farmers Club (Hampapura branch, H.D.Kote Taluk) has been awarded as the best farmers club for the year 2005-06 by NABARD among the Farmers Club in Karnataka.

Financial Inclusion

This is the second mass banking movement after micro-finance/SHGs. The bank therefore has taken up earnest steps to promote financial inclusion of low-income groups treating it both as a business opportunity as well as a corporate social responsibility.

Recovery of Loans

During the year, more emphasis was laid on recovery, continuous follow up and supervision of branches was made where recovery per centage is low. Repayment camps, repayment awareness camps, intensive recovery drives were conducted in all branches. Branches were allotted to all the officers at Head Office for intensive monitoring of recovery. Hired vehicles were provided to cover more number of borrowers during harvest season. For the DCB year ended June 2009, the recovery per centage showed an increase of 8.64% from 73.06% to 81.70%. During the financial year

2008-09, bank has recovered an amount of Rs.175.79 crore against budgeted target of Rs.163 crore. The recovery of loans issued by Cauvery Grameena Bank is furnished in the Table 5.11.

Table 5.11
Recovery of Loans

Segment	*June 2008*			*June 2009*		
	D	*C*	*B*	*D*	*C*	*B*
STL AGL	1731.38	1303.53	427.85	3937.12	3279.90	657.22
Agriculture Term Loan	1725.48	836.62	888.86	2163.77	1379.43	784.34
Total Farm Sector	3456.86	2140.15	1316.71	6100.89	4659.33	1441.56
Non-Farm Sector	2313.24	1866.50	446.74	4110.05	3580.67	29.38
Total Priority Sector	5770.10	4006.65 (69.44)	1763.45	10210.94	8240.00 (80.70)	1970.94
Non-priority Sector	1071.06	991.21 (92.54)	79.85	1128.16	1029.20 (91.23)	98.96
Grand Total	684116	4997.86 (73.06)	1843.30	11339.10	9269.20 (81.75)	2069.90

Source: Annual Reports, Cauvery Grameena Bank.

Important Strategies Adopted for Recovery

1. Area Managers, Recovery Officers and all officers working at Head Office including Chairmen and General Managers were allotted branches to effectively monitor the NPA accounts and also potential NPA accounts from July 2005 itself.
2. Identification of NPAs well in advance in January 2009, which was intensively monitored for recovery by the Area Offices on account to account basis.
3. Targets fixed to the branches for NPA recoveries.

4. Monthly monitoring of Rs. 50,000 and above accounts which are due for renewal/recovery of installments.
5. During the year 2008-09, the bank experimented the Bank Adalat in 62 branches. The following strategies were adopted to ensure success of Bank Adalat.
   (A) Conducting a preliminary meeting of the well-wishers of the bank drawn from villages where NPA accounts are existing and explaining the interest concession available and also fixing the date of bank adalat in consultation with them.
   (B) With the support of these well wishers who are VVV club members, SHG members or informal leaders of the villages, contacted each of the defaulters, explained the interest concession available and the benefits of OTS and convince them to avail the opportunity and handed over notice of bank adalat.
   (C) Follow-up these accounts few more times before adalat.

The efforts yielded good results, as the bank was able to recover Rs. 1.23 crore under written off accounts, which is highest besides significant recovery of NPAs.

Cauvery Grameena Bank has controlled it operational expenses quite efficiently, though the working results reveals excess of expenditure over its income in all years. The gap between income and expenditure is quite small. Bank has taken many steps towards reduce the NPAs. Recently the bank has been merged with another bank i.e., Cauvery Grameena Bank.

An attempt has been made in this chapter to present a general picture of some of the major findings of the study, major problems and constraints faced by the regional rural banks. Regional Rural Banks are specialized rural financial institutions for catering to the credit needs of the rural sector. Even though the RRBs are providing better services to the rural poor, they have only limited resources and concentrate on a small geographical area. This is the time of globalization, in the globalised world; the Indian banks face competition from the foreign banks. The RRBs face competition from other PSCBs and also from private sector banks. It creates undue competition among the banks under the same ownership.

The purpose of setting up the RRBs is to prepare and develop a rural economy through disbursement of credit and other accommodations, especially to small and marginal farmers, agricultural labourers, artisans and small entrepreneurs. The RRBs are expected to combine the local feel and the low cost of cooperatives on the one and managerial competence of the commercial banks on the other.

There is no doubt that credit is important and constitutes the key-element in the share of almost every economy activity. Credit plays a vital role in agricultural progress. Indian rural people do not have funds of their own to carry out their agricultural operations, ranging from ploughing to marketing of the produce. They have not been able to secure adequate and cheap finance for their seasonal agricultural operations or for making permanent improvements to land.

To bring about overall development in the rural areas, financial assistance to the rural poor particularly institutional assistance needs boosting. Small and marginal farmers constitute bulk of the rural population; these categories are not in a position to improve their economic conditions and income levels because of the low investment capacity. Providing credit may lead to create employment and income and may lead to the agricultural development and pave the way for achieving the desired objective of rural development. If required finance is not available out of ones own income, then one is forced to seek external source of finance i.e., credit. Rural population mainly constitutes agricultural producers, tenant cultivators, village artisans, land less labour etc., all these categories most of the times are in need of credit.

To meet the credit requirements of rural people in Mysore district, Cauvery Grameena Bank was established. Cauvery Grameena Bank has so far been able to achieve the objective of helping the weaker sections despite the constraints. Cauvery Grameena Bank within the reasonable limits has been doing its best to maximize the lendings to small entrepreneurs and persons engaged in service sector. The main objective of this bank has been to provide credit and other facilities especially to the small and marginal farmers, agricultural labourers, artisans and small entrepreneurs in rural areas. The numbers of accounts have also been increased rapidly.

Bank's credit operations are closely inter-linked with IRDP/SGSY programmes and allied programmes and thereby it is able to make significant contribution to rural development. Cauvery Grameena Bank's record in mobilisation of savings, disbursement of advances as well as recovery of loans is impressive with its wide coverage in the district.

Though the progress of the Cauvery Grameena Bank in terms of deposits, advances and in other aspects is commendable, still it appears that there are certain gaps in the effective functioning of Cauvery Grameena Bank.

Problems in Issuing the Credit

Cauvery Grameena Bank is being faced a few problems while issuing the credit to the beneficiaries. Some important problems are:

(A) Identification of the right type of borrowers who are really in need of finance is a serious problem faced by this bank. Further, the borrowers seem to be of the impression that the Cauvery Grameena Bank on par with other institutional agencies would waive the loans granted to them. This type of impressions with other factors has resulted in increasing the magnitude of overdues. As such this is evident need that farmers must be educated and the habit of repayment of the loans as scheduled be inculcated.

(B) It is found that only 45 per cent of the borrowers are paying regular installments of the loan amount. Identification of borrowers who can honestly repay the loan amount was a crucial problem faced by the bank staff. Wrong selection of borrowers was and has been resulting in mounting overdues and losses to the bank. The borrowers are under the wrong impression that the bank loans are aided money and hence need not be repaid. This attitude further increases the number of willful defaulters.

Case Study Analysis

A detailed analysis of the impact of bank credit on the income level of the beneficiaries and the status of the beneficiaries has been studied from various angles like category of beneficiary, economic status, level of education, age group of beneficiaries, size of household and social category.

Block-wise and Activity-wise Distribution of Respondents

On the whole, 250 respondents of Cauvery Grameena Bank who were financed under various schemes were interviewed for the study. Table 5.12 presents block-wise and sector-wise distribution of sample respondents. It can be observed that out of 250 respondents selected for this study 50 (20%) respondents are from crop loans, 50 (20%) respondents from tractor loan; 50 (20%) respondents from digging wells loans 50 (20%) respondents from dairy activity; and 50 (20%) respondents from bullock carts loans. In Mysore block, the maximum number of respondents (27.27%) is from crop loans and the minimum (11.37%) from bullockcarts loans. In T.N. Pura block, the largest number (24.09%) of respondents is from digging wells and bullock carts loans and the smallest number (16.88) from tractor loans. In K.R.Nagara block, the maximum number of respondents (29.12%) are from dairy activity and the minimum number (7.60%) from digging wells.

In Mysore block 88 respondents, 83 respondents from T.N. Pura, 79 respondents from K.R. Nagara are being selected for the study from five important activities. The activities like crop loans, tractor loans, digging wells, dairy activity and bullock carts.

Table 5.12
Block-wise and Activity-wise Distribution of Sample Respondents

Sl. No	*Activity*	*Block*			
		Mysore	*T.N.Pura*	*K.R.Nagara*	*Total*
1.	Crop loans	24 (27.27)	15 (18.07)	15 (18.98)	50 (20%)
2	Tractor loans	21 (23.87)	14 (16.88)	15 (18.98)	50 (20%)
3	Digging wells	20 (22.72)	20 (24.09)	06 (7.60)	50 (20%)
4	Dairy activity	13 (14.77)	14 (16.88)	23 (29.12)	50 (20%)
5	Bullockcarts loans	10 (11.37)	20 (24.09)	20 (25.32)	50 (20%)
	Total Activity	**88 (100%)**	**83 (100%)**	**79 (100%)**	**250 (100%)**

Source: Field Survey.

Note: Figures in brackets represent per cent share of each activity.

Activity-wise Distribution of Respondents

Table 5.13 offers activity-wise distribution of sample respondents.

It can be said that, out of 250 respondents interviewed, 50 (20%) obtained loan for agriculture purpose as crop loans. Other items are 50 (20%) obtained loan for tractor purpose, for digging wells 50 respondents obtained, 50 (20%) obtained loan from RRBs for dairy activity and 50 respondents got financial assistance to purchase of bullockcarts.

Table 5.13
Activity-wise Distribution of Respondents

Sl. No	*Activity*	*Number of respondents*	*Overall per centage*
1.	Crop loans	50	20
2.	Tractor loans	50	20
3.	Digging wells	50	20
4.	Dairy activity	50	20
5.	Bullockcarts loans	50	20
	Total Activity	**250**	100

Source: Field Survey.

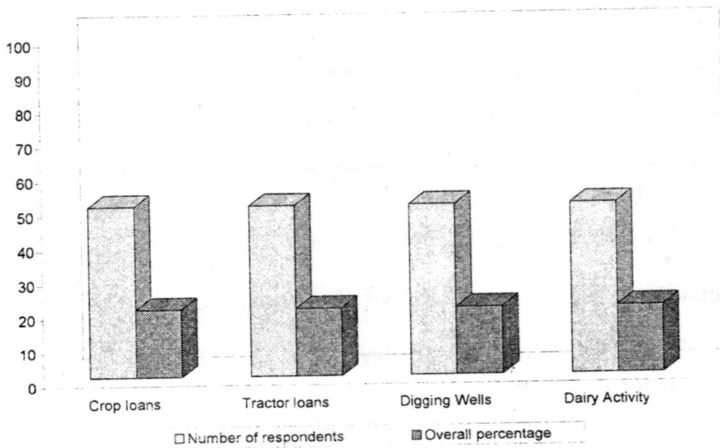

Age Group of Sample Respondents

In social science research age of the respondents is considered to be an important determinant of the progressive nature of a person. It is generally felt that after attaining a certain age, a person may not be responsive to the new ideas and become somewhat conversative. Age-wise distribution of the sample respondents has been depicted in the Table 5.14.

Table- 5.14
Age-wise Distribution of Sample Respondents

Sl. No	*Age-group*	*Respondents*	*Per cent*
1.	Below 40	110	44.00
2.	40 - 45	102	40.80
3.	45 - 50	38	15.20
	Total	**250**	**100**

Source: Field Survey.

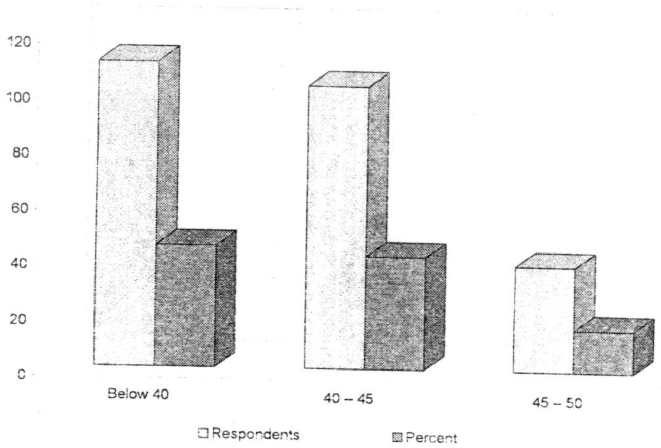

From the above table it is clear that below 40 age group are the maximum beneficiaries and 45-50 age group are the minimum respondents. Youngsters were benefited maximum by the regional rural banks loans. Below 40 age group respondents 110 (44%), 40 – 50 age group respondents were 102 (40.80%) and between 45 – 50 age group respondents were only 38 (15.20%). This trend shows that young farmers are very much eager to seek financial assistance of the grameen banks. This is very much required also, because there is need to strengthen the young farmers also in order to strengthen the agriculture sector thereby reduce the unemployment.

Social Category-wise Distribution of Respondents

The details of social category also very much important. Because to know the dominance of caste in a social stratification country like India caste dominance is significant, in such an economy how social justice is maintained by the public institutions inorder to reduce income inequality, wealth redistribution etc. Table 5.15 portrays the distribution of the sample respondents on the basis of their social category. Out of 250 beneficiaries under study 79.2 per cent are from Hindu and 14.8 per cent respondents are from Muslim and only 6 per cent are from Jain religion. The main reason for this may be that Hindu especially Gowda and Lingayath caste people dominates while availing the bank loans, and another reason may be that Lingayath community in the Mysore district playing a dominant role to help their village weaker sections during the sanction of loan, the main intention is vote banking.

Table 5.15

Religion-wise Distribution of Sample Respondents

Sl. No	*Religion*	*Respondents*	*Per cent*
1.	Hindu	198	79.2
2.	Muslim	37	14.8
3.	Jain	15	6.0
	Total	250	100

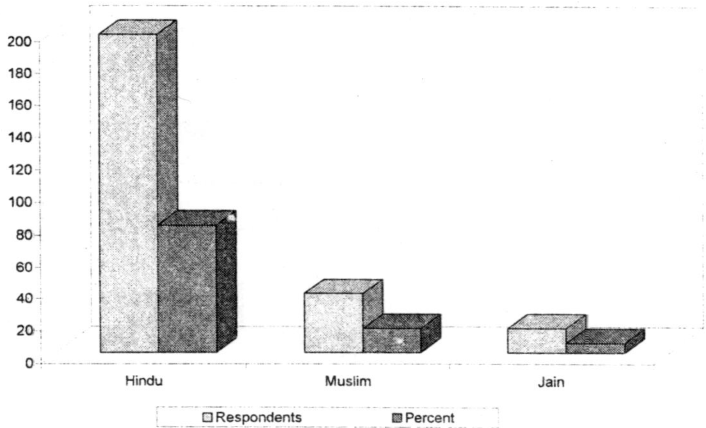

Table 5.16 indicates that the caste-wise distribution of sample respondents. Out of 250 sample respondents under study, 8.0 per cent respondents belong to scheduled caste; 7.6 per cent respondents belong to scheduled tribes; 30 per cent respondents are from vokkaliga community; 32 per cent respondents are from lingayath community; 14 per cent of the respondents are from other backward classes; and 8.4 per cent of the respondents are from minorities.It is important to note that, the maximum number of loaners belonging to lingayath and vokkaliga community. However, a sizable number of loaners of other backward classes and minorities.

Table 5.16
Social Category-wise Distribution of Sample Respondents

Sl. No	*Category*	*Respondents*	*Per cent*
1.	Scheduled caste	20	8.0
2.	Scheduled tribe	19	7.6
3.	Vokkaliga	75	30.0
4.	Lingayath	80	32.0
5.	Other backward classes	35	14.0
6.	Minorities	21	8.4
	Total	**250**	**100**

Source: Field Survey.

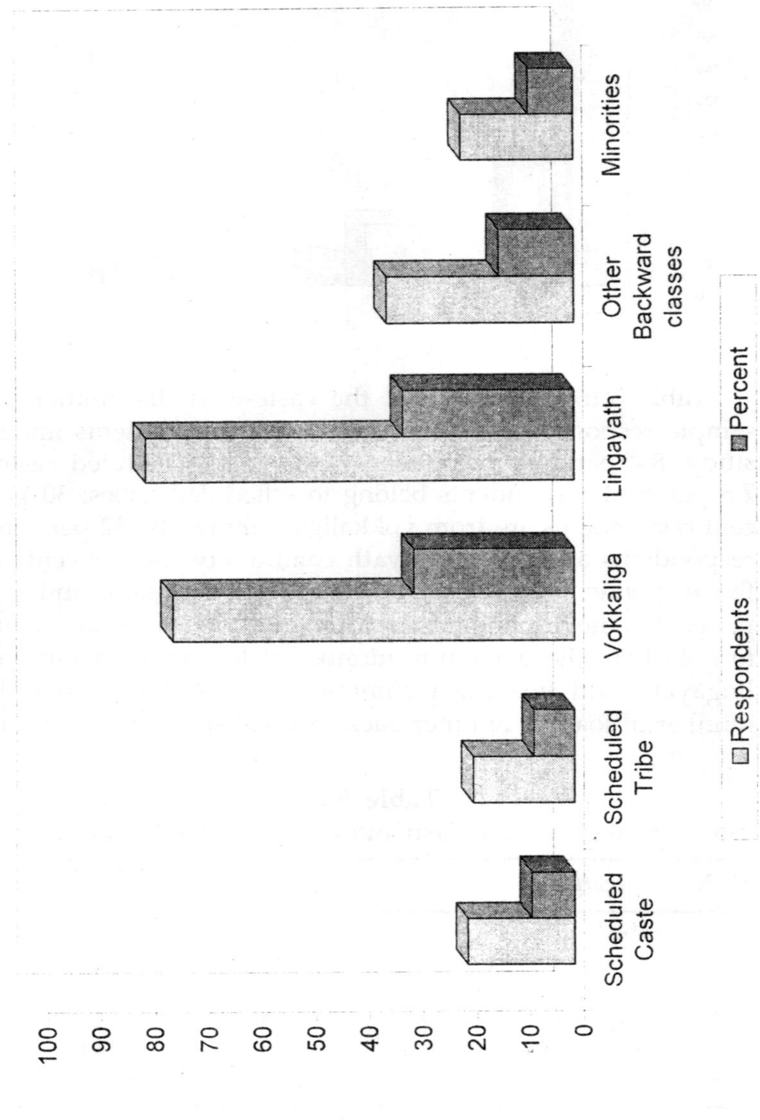
100
90
80
70
60
50
40
30
20
10
0
Scheduled Caste
Scheduled Tribe
Vokkaliga
Lingayath
Other Backward classes
Minorities
Respondents
Percent

Educational Level of the Respondents

Education is an important determinant factor of development. Education plays the role a means for human resource development for sensitizing one's perceptions, awareness and for motivating and changing one's behaviour to suit arising needs, demands and opportunities for survival, growth and development. It is the greatest force for development. So to enable the agriculturists to obtain loan from financial institutions the government should implementation much more programmes to educate the farmers to know about the government programmes for upliftment of the agriculture sector. The literacy standard of the sample respondents has been given in Table 5.17. In all 14 per cent of the respondents can read and write (can put their signature) where as 32.8 per cent of the loaners have SSLC level education, 34.8 per cent of the respondents have PUC level education and 18.4 per cent of the respondents have Degree and above education. It is evident that more than 85 per cent of the loaners of all the sectors are literates, 14 per cent of the loaners can read and write. Very interesting point is that no beneficiary is illiterate among the 250 sample respondents selected for the survey.

Table 5.17
Education Level of the Sample Respondents

Sl. No	*Education level*	*Respondents*	*Per cent*
1.	Can read and write	35	14.0
2.	SSLC	82	32.8
3.	PUC	87	34.8
4.	Degree and above	46	18.4
	Total	**250**	**100**

Source: Field Survey.

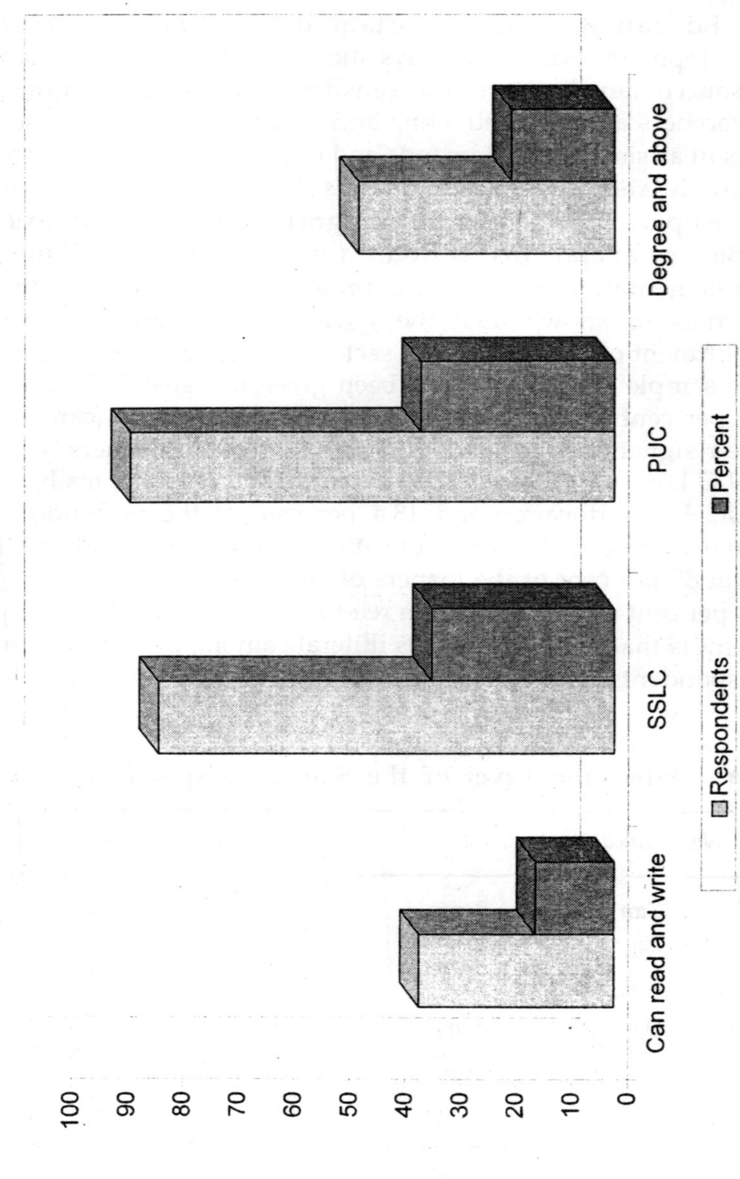
100
90
80
70
60
50
40
30
20
10
0
Can read and write
SSLC
PUC
Degree and above
Respondents
Percent

Nature of Loan Provided by Grameen Bank

Table 5.18 provides the details of the nature of loan provided by the Cauvery Grameena Bank for the farming community in Mysore district. Nature of loan of farmers includes three categories;

1. Short-term loans;
2. Medium-term loans; and
3. Long-term loans.

Out of 250 respondents, 70 per cent of the respondents provided short-term loan; 18 per cent of the respondents provided medium-term loans and only 12 per cent of the respondents provided long-term loans, in the study area. It is pertinent to note that all type of loans have been provided by the grameen bank in the district.

Table 5.18
Nature of Loan Provided by Cauvery Grameena Bank

Sl. No	*Mode of loan*	*Respondents*	*Per cent*
1.	Short-term	175	70.0
2.	Medium-term	45	18.0
3.	Long-term	30	12.0
	Total	**250**	**100**

Source: Filed Survey.

Amount of Loan Required

The details of the amount of loan required by sample respondents have been given in Table 5.19. Out of 250 sample respondents 40 per cent reported the loan required amount of Rs. 25,000 and 60 per cent of the respondents reported Rs. 50,000 loan amount. In all, 72 per cent loaners are recipients of loan for an amount not exceeding Rs. 20,000. This is perhaps

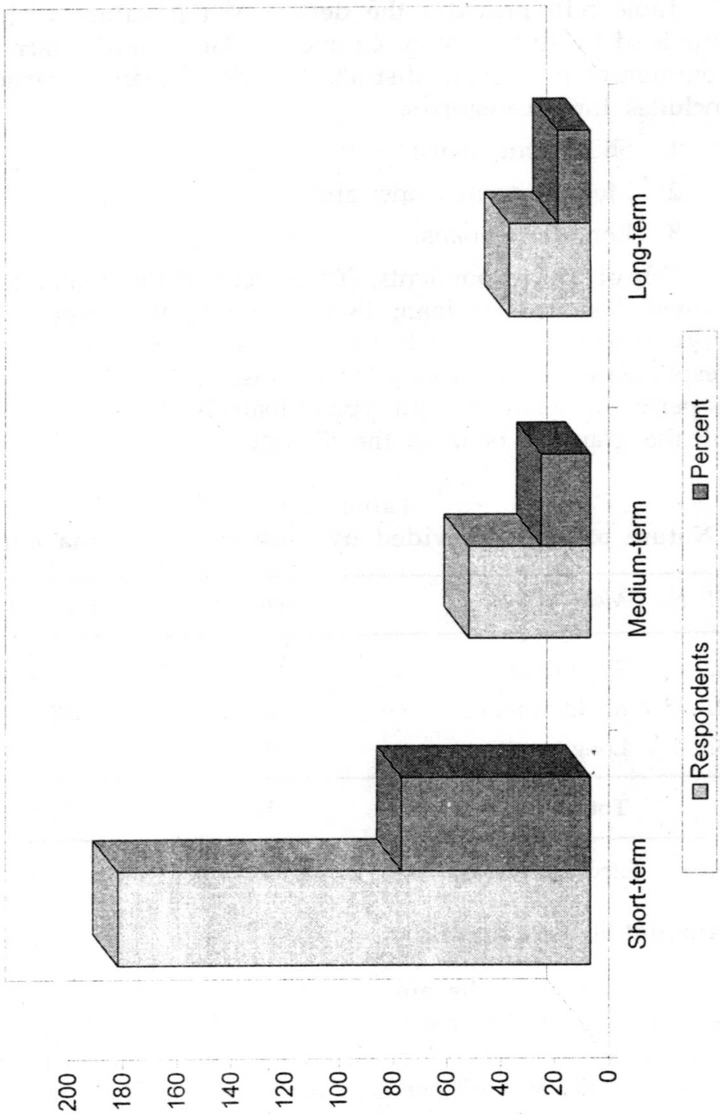
200
180
160
140
120
100
80
60
40
20
0
Short-term
Medium-term
Long-term
Respondents
Percent

because agricultural loans up to Rs. 20,000 are advanced without any mortgage of property as security of loan; moreover under most of the loans sponsored by various agencies, the project cost does not exceed Rs. 20,000.

Table 5.19
Distribution of Respondents According to Amount of Loan

Sl. No	*Amount of loan required*	*Respondents*	*Per cent*
1.	Rs. 25,000	100	40.0
2.	Rs. 50,000	150	60.0
	Total	**250**	**100**
3.	Rs. up to 20,000	195	78.0
4.	Rs. up to 35,000	55	22.0
	Total	**250**	**100**

Source: Field Survey.

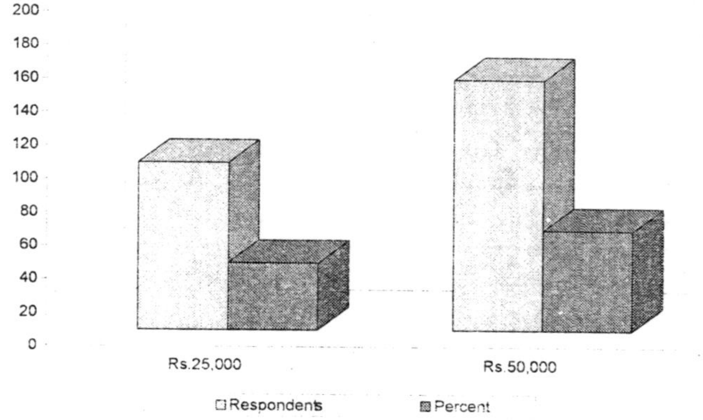

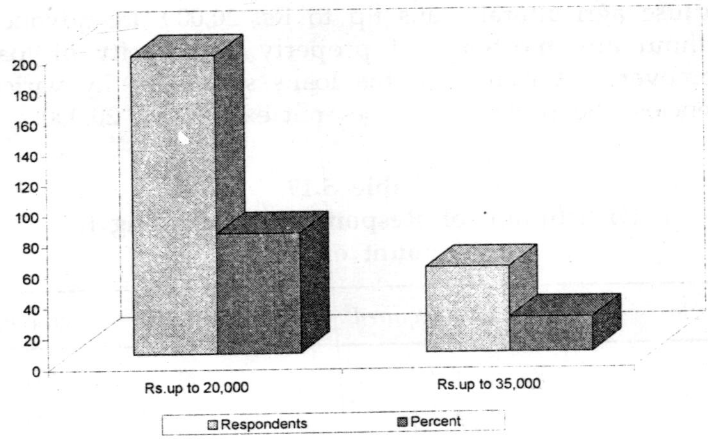

Reasons for Seeking Bank Loans

Out of the 250 sample respondents covered under study, 40.8 per cent respondents took bank loans for starting the activity; this is the major reason was given by respondents. For the 32.8 per cent respondents the intention to expand the scale of activity was another major reason for taking the bank loans. And another third major reason was the attraction of low interest on loans under the social purpose lending schemes (i.e.15.6 per cent respondents). The fourth reason was to avoid taking loans from intermediaries (i.e. 10.8 per cent respondents). The details can be seen in Table 5.20.

Table 5.20
Reasons for Seeking Bank Loans

Sl. No	*Reasons*	*Respondents*	*Per cent*
1.	To start activity	102	40.8
2.	To expand the activity	82	32.8
3.	To avaii of low interest finance	39	15.6
4.	To eliminate intermediary	27	10.8
	Total	**250**	**100**

Source: Field Survey.

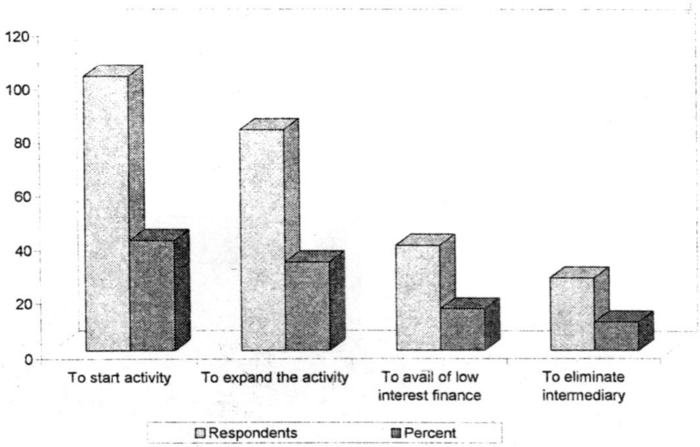

Inadequacy of Bank Loan

Inadequate amount of loan affects its proper utilization to a great extent. This inadequacy often either leads to unproductive spending and in the long run, may turnout to be counter-productive and defeating the very objective of financing or compels the poor respondents to knock at the door of the professional money lenders. To save the weaker sections (poor farmers) from falling into the clutches of the private money lenders, it would be necessary for the banks to provide adequate amount of loan.

Table 5.21
Inadequacy of Bank Loan Amount

Sl. No	*Particulars*	*No.of respondents*	*Per cent*
1.	Adequate	102	40.8
2.	Inadequate	148	59.2
	Total	**250**	**100**

Source: Field Survey.

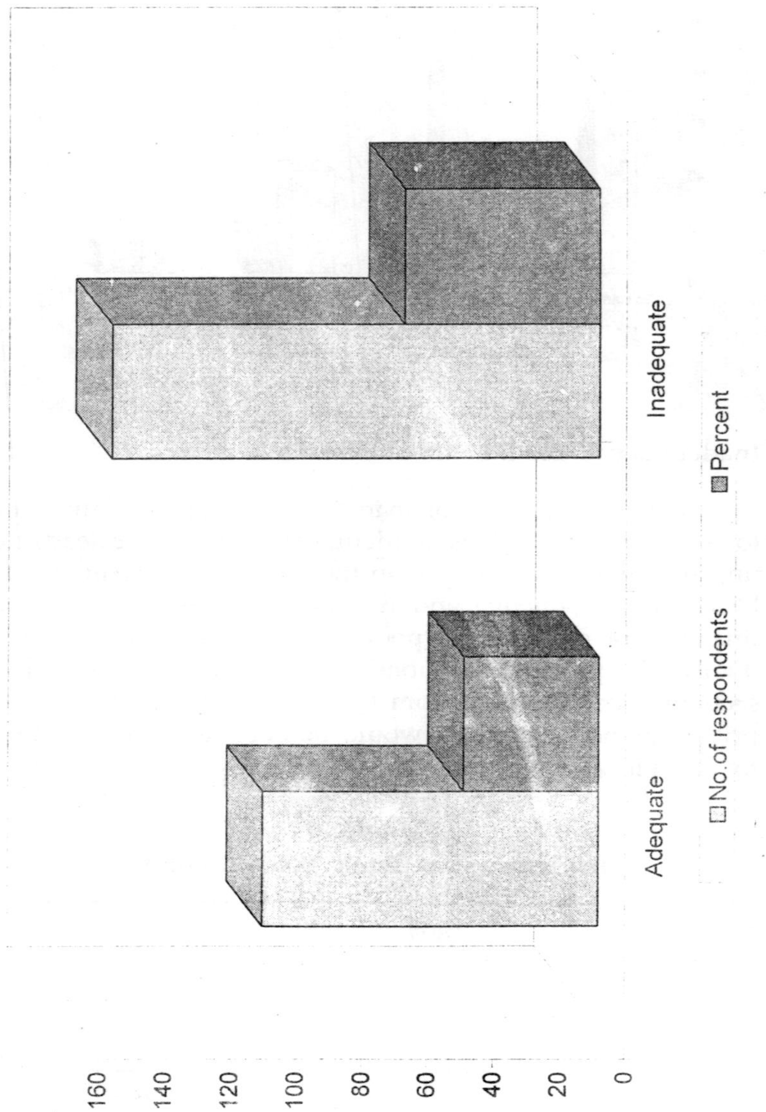
160
140
120
100
80
60
40
20
0
Adequate
Inadequate
No.of respondents
Percent

Table 5.21 depicts that in 59.2 per cent cases the amount of bank loan was found to be inadequate for the activity and in only 40.8 per cent cases it was adequate. This opinion is usually opined by small farmers, this amount is enough to maintain their activity. But in the case of large farmers or those who are intends to go for digging wells and purchasing bullock costs this amount is not adequate.

Diversion of bank loan

Table - 5.22 analyses data concerning diversion of loan amount by the sample respondents. Out of 250 sample respondents 57.2 per cent loaners have used the loan amount for the purpose it was borrowed, but the remaining 42.8 per cent loaners used the amount of loan for a purpose other than that for which it was provided. The analysis of the reasons for diversion of loan makes it clear that 11.6 per cent loaners diverted the loan amount towards private

Table 5.22
Reasons for Diversion of Loan by Sample Respondents

Sl. No	*Reasons*	*Respondents*	*Per cent*
1.	Amount spent on social ceremonies	11	4.4
2.	Amount spent on private consumption	29	11.6
3.	Repayment of old debts	11	4.4
4.	Inadequate loan amount	12	4.8
5.	Delay in disbursement of loan	13	5.2
6.	Amount used in better manner	25	10.0
7.	Other reasons	6	2.4
8.	No diversion	143	57.2
	Total	**250**	**100**

Source: Field Survey.

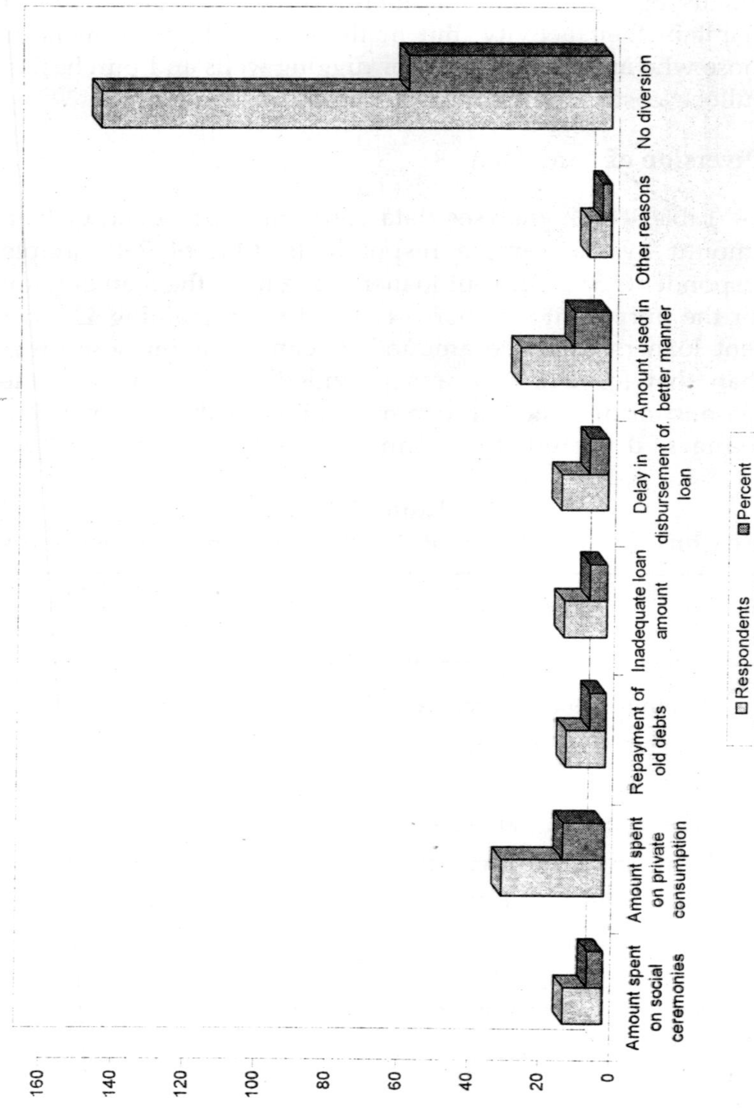
0
20
40
60
80
100
120
140
160
Amount spent on social ceremonies
Amount spent on private consumption
Repayment of old debts
Inadequate loan amount
Delay in disbursement of loan
Amount used in better manner
Other reasons
No diversion
Respondents
Percent

consumption; 10 per cent loaners used the loan amount in better manner; 4.4 per cent loaners made the diversion of loan for repayment of old debt and also spent on social ceremonies; 5.2 per cent loaners delay in disbursement of loan resulted in diversion of loan; in 4.8 per cent loaners owing to inadequacy of loan amount; and in 2.4 per cent cases diversion was due to other reasons.

It may be noted that the most important reason for diversion of loan is, it is spent on private consumption and repayment of old debt. The analysis brings to light that the pressing need of private consumption is one of the main reasons for diversion of loan. Therefore, it would be better if loaners of weaker sections were also provided consumption loans in addition to productive loans. Moreover, inadequacy of loan amount and require due attention of the agencies involved in poverty alleviation programmes.

Reasons for Default

Regular and timely recovery of bank loan is considered to be an important parameter to test the degree of success of a social banking programme. Recovery of loan is very closely related to generation of adequate income. According to Table 5.23, out of 250 sample respondents, 57.2 per cent did not make any default and the remaining 42.8 per cent made default in repayment of loan for one reason or the other. The most significant point to note is that, in the maximum cases of default, the loaners are willful defaulters. Nearly 11.6 per cent respondents are willful defaulters, 8.8 per cent is insufficient income from the activity financed; and another reason for default of loan is adverse family circumstances. Another important reason for default is the hope for loan moratorium. It was found during field study that loaners did not pay loan installments because they were hopeful that their loans were going to be written off.

Table 5.23
Reasons for Default by Sample Respondents

Sl. No	*Reasons*	*Respondents*	*Per cent*
1.	Willful	29	11.6
2.	Insufficient income from the activity financed	22	8.8
3.	Adverse family circumstances	16	6.4
4.	Non-follow up by bank officials	12	4.8
5.	Hoping for loan writing off	28	11.2
6.	No default	143	57.2
	Total	**250**	**100**

Source: Field Survey.

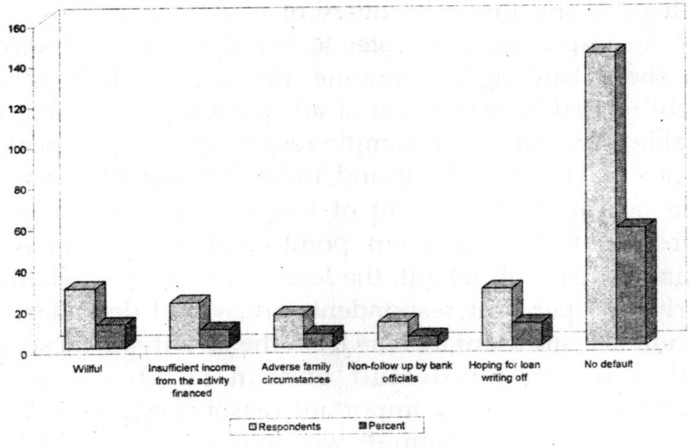

The scheme of debt relief was found to have adverse effect on repayment performance of the loaners. Under this scheme, no benefit was given to the loaners who were regularly paying the installments due, but the loaners who never visited bank office after obtaining bank loan and were chronic defaulters were lucky enough to get their dues written off.

The analysis of the reasons for default by sample respondents makes it clear that, leaving aside the cases where loaners could not get sufficient income from activity financed, the loaners, by and large, were able to repay the bank loan out of the incremental income from activity financed. The willful default is most striking reason for non-repayment of bank credit.

Impact of Bank Credit on Farming Community

Creation of employment opportunities and generation of adequate income for the beneficiaries is the theme of all social banking programmes. The endeavour is to lift the weakest among the weaker sections of the society above the poverty line on a permanent basis. This part is devoted to the analysis of the impact of bank credit on the income level of the beneficiaries, and to gauge the extent to which financing under various social banking schemes, programmes were successful in fulfilling the objectives laid-down before the banking industry.

The increase in income level and thereby improvement in the economic conditions of the beneficiaries, after the bank loans, was possible due to the favourable changes in the arrangements for procurement of inputs. The bank loans enabled them to become independent and to realize higher profit margin for their product.

It is evident from the Table 5.24 that average amount of post-loan income is substantially higher than pre-loan income for all the activities under study. In this sector, average pre-loan income is Rs. 4096.15, which has risen to Rs. 6144.23 in the post-loan period. There are 21 respondents with pre-loan income range between Rs. 3000 to Rs. 5000 who were not able to improve their income. There is one beneficiary in the income Rs. 5500 who is able to improve his income in post-loan period.

The number of loaners in the income ranges Rs. 6500 to Rs. 9000 is 30 in the post-loan period. There is increase in the number of respondents in the higher income levels in the post-loan period. Median income of agricultural loaners indicates that 58 per cent of th . loaners of this sector are getting income above Rs. 7000 in the post-loan period. The dispersion in income of the loaners is slightly higher in the post-loan period as compared to the pre-loan period.

Agricultural Crop

Among the agricultural sector respondents, increase in income actually represents the saving of interest amount by availing bank credit and paying interest at a lower rate than they would have paid, had they borrowed the same amount from agricultural money-lenders. The beneficiaries of tractor loans, on the other hand, were able to increase their income to a great extent.

A significantly positive correlation between pre-loan income and post-loan income establishes the point that those who had higher pre-loan income had higher income in the post-loan period as well. It can be inferred that those respondents who were using their own resources in the best possible manner and getting higher income were also in a position to earn a lot by using bank assistance.

Table 5.24
Crop Loan Respondents: Pre-loan Income

Sl. No	*Amount (Rs.)*	*Respondents*	*Per cent*
1.	3000	10	20.00
2.	3500	3	6.00
3.	4000	14	28.00
4.	4500	12	24.00
5.	5000	11	22.00
	Total	**50**	**100**

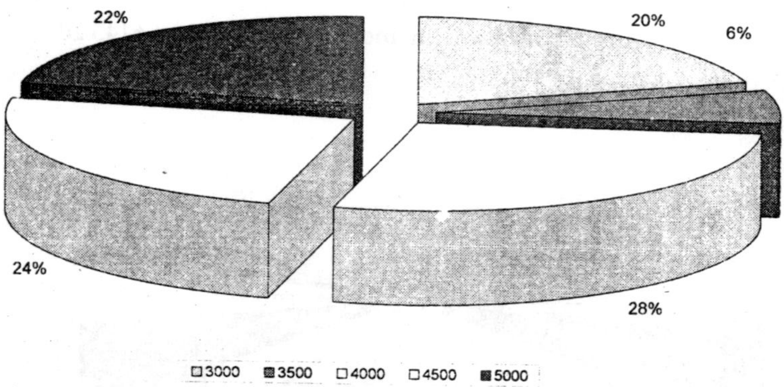

Average amount of increase in income: (Rs.) Mean: 4095.14 Median: 4000.

Crop Loan Respondents: Post- Loan Income

Sl. No	*Amount (Rs)*	*Respondents*	*Per cent*
1.	3000	7	14.00
2.	3500	2	4.00
3.	4000	4	8.00
4.	4500	2	4.00
5.	5000	5	10.00
6.	5500	2	4.00
7.	6500	2	4.00
8.	7000	6	12.00
9.	7500	4	8.00
10.	8000	3	6.00
11.	8500	7	14.00
12.	9000	6	12.00
	Total	**50**	**100.00**

Average amount of increase in income: (Rs) Mean: 6143.20
Median: 7000

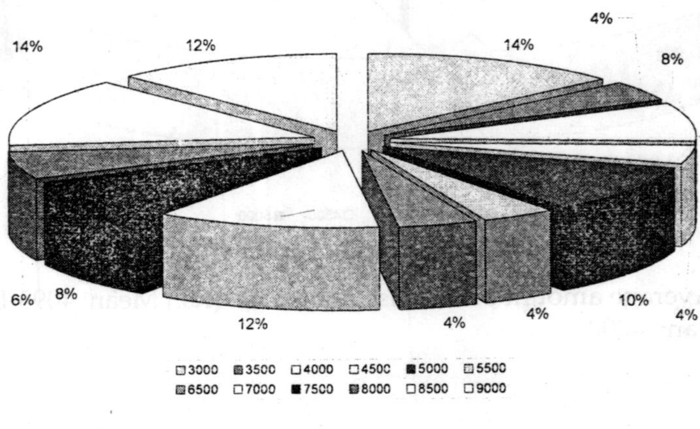

Impact on Respondents of Tractor Loaners

In this activity, above 70 per cent of respondents pertain to tractor loans. Table 5.25 indicates that, there are 15 respondents with pre-loan income range between Rs. 5000 to Rs.7500 who are not able to improve their income after bank loans. The number of loaners in the income ranges between Rs.9000 to Rs.15000 is 34 in the post-loan period. This clearly shows that there is an increasing trend in the number of beneficiaries in the higher income levels in the post-loan period. Out of 50 beneficiaries selected under study 34 respondents have been improved their income. Median income of tractor loaners indicates that 70 per cent of the loaners of this activity are getting income above Rs. 10000 in the post-loan period.

Tractor

Table 5.25

Tractor Loaners: Pre-Loan Period

Sl. No.	*Amount (Rs)*	*Respondents*	*Per cent*
1.	5000	18	36.00
2.	6500	15	30.00
3.	7500	17	34.00
	Total	**50**	**100.00**

Average amount of increase in income: (Rs) Mean: 6271.82 Median: 6500.

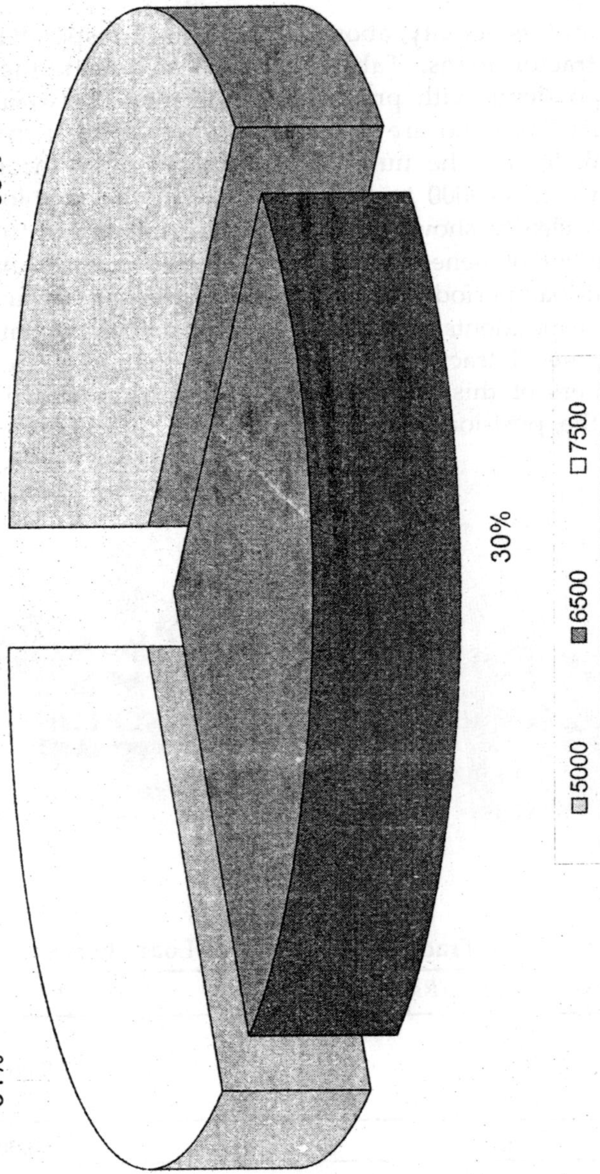
36%
34%
30%
5000
6500
7500

Tractor Loaners: Post-Loan Period

Sl. No	*Amount (Rs.)*	*Respondents*	*Per cent*
1.	5000	11	22.00
2.	6500	03	6.00
3.	7500	02	4.00
4.	9000	06	12.00
5.	10000	14	28.00
6.	12000	06	12.00
7.	15000	08	16.00
	Total	**50**	**100.00**

Average amount of increase in income: (Rs) Mean: 9615.56 Median: 10000.

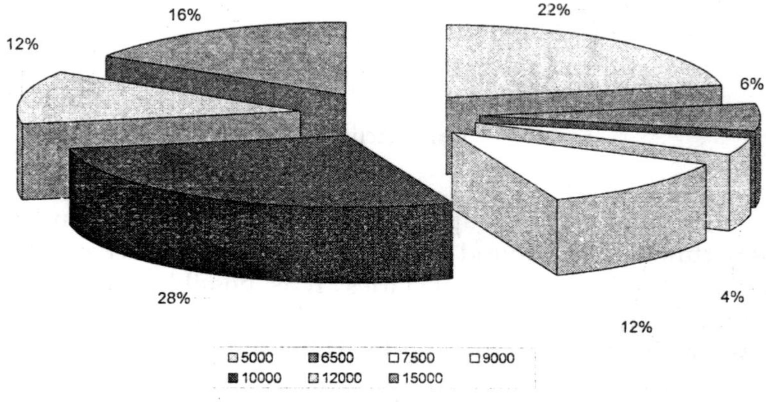

Impact on Beneficiaries of Dairy

It has been observed during the course of the study that in cases of direct financing by banks for the purchase of two buffaloes giving a gap of six months of the beneficiaries were able to get a continuous flow of income, resulting in repayment of loans and better income effect on the beneficiary.

Dairy Activity

The dairy loans sponsored by animal husbandry department were found to have impressive effect on the income level of the beneficiaries. It is possible because of training imparted to the borrowers before sponsoring their cases to banks for providing loans. Some beneficiaries took up another allied to agriculture, namely piggery. By and large, the beneficiaries of this activity earned a good return because of low cost for running the activity. The details can be seen from Table 5.26.

Table 5.26
Dairy Loaners: Pre-Loan Period

Sl. No	*Amount (Rs.)*	*Respondents*	*Per cent*
1.	10000	15	30.00
2.	12000	19	38.00
3.	15000	16	32.00

Average amount of increase in income: (Rs) Mean: 12256.80 Median: 12000.

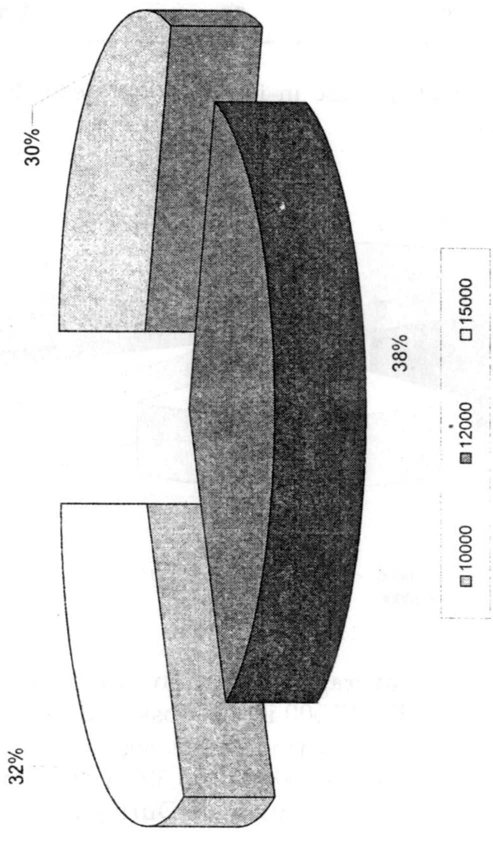

Dairy Loaners: Post-Loan Period

Sl. No	*Amount(Rs)*	*Respondents*	*Per cent*
1.	10000	10	20.00
2.	12000	6	12.00
3.	15000	4	8.00
4.	17500	11	22.00
5.	20000	11	22.00
6.	25000	8	16.00
	Total	**50**	**100.00**

Average amount of increase in income: (Rs) Mean: 16942.85 Median: 17500.

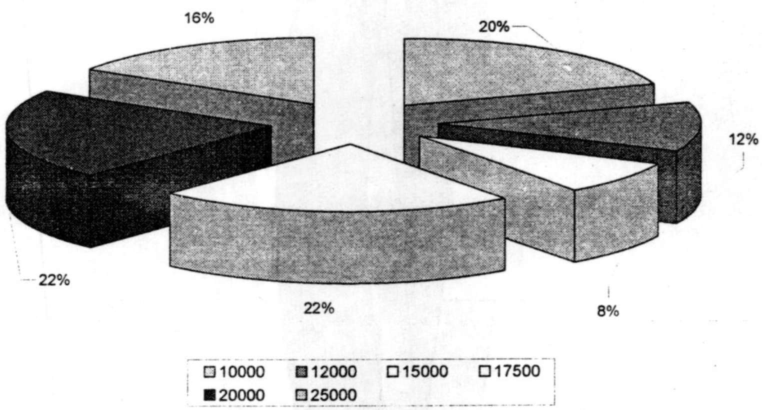

In this activity, average pre-loan income is Rs. 12,256.80, which has risen to Rs. 17,500 in the post-loan period. Median income during pre-loan period of this sector was Rs. 12,000. Hence, it is clearly shows that Rs.5,500 is the incremental income after obtaining the bank loan. During post-loan period

Median income of this sector was Rs.17,500. This shows that increasing tendency after taking loan from the Grameena Bank.

Impact on Bullockcarts Beneficiaries

Table 5.27 would enable us to appreciate the role played by regional rural banks in improving the income levels of the loaners of bullockcarts. It can be observed that a beneficiary, irrespective of age, family size, number of literate in the family, debts of the family, amount of loan and supplementary investment in the activity, can be successful in this activity. In this activity, average pre-loan income is Rs.12,255.81 which has risen to Rs.16,941.86 is the post-loan period. Median income of this activity loaners indicates that 65.2 per cent of the loaners of this sector are getting income above Rs.17,500 in the post-loan period. Median income during pre-loan period of this sector was Rs.12,000. Hence it is clearly shows that Rs.5,500 rupees is the incremental income after obtaining the bank loan.

Bullockcarts

Table 5.27

Bullockcarts Activity Loaners: Pre-loan Period

Sl. No	*Amount (Rs.)*	*Respondents*	*Per cent*
1.	10000	15	30.00
2.	12000	17	34.00
3.	15000	18	36.00
	Total	**50**	**100.00**

Average amount of increase in income: (Rs.) Mean: 12,255.81 Median: 12,000.

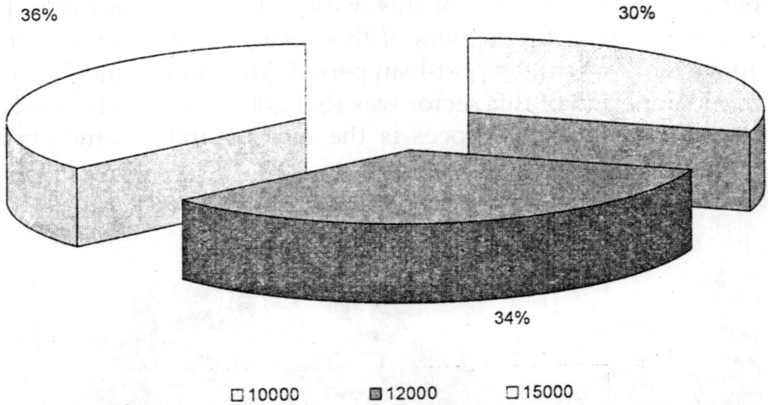

Bullockcarts Activity Loaners: Post-loan Period

Sl. No	*Amount(Rs)*	*Respondents*	*Per cent*
1.	10000	10	20.00
2.	12000	5	10.00
3.	15000	4	8.00
4.	17500	12	24.00
5.	20000	12	24.00
6.	25000	7	14.00
	Total	50	**100.00**

Average amount of increase in income: (Rs) Mean: 16941.86 Median: 17,500.

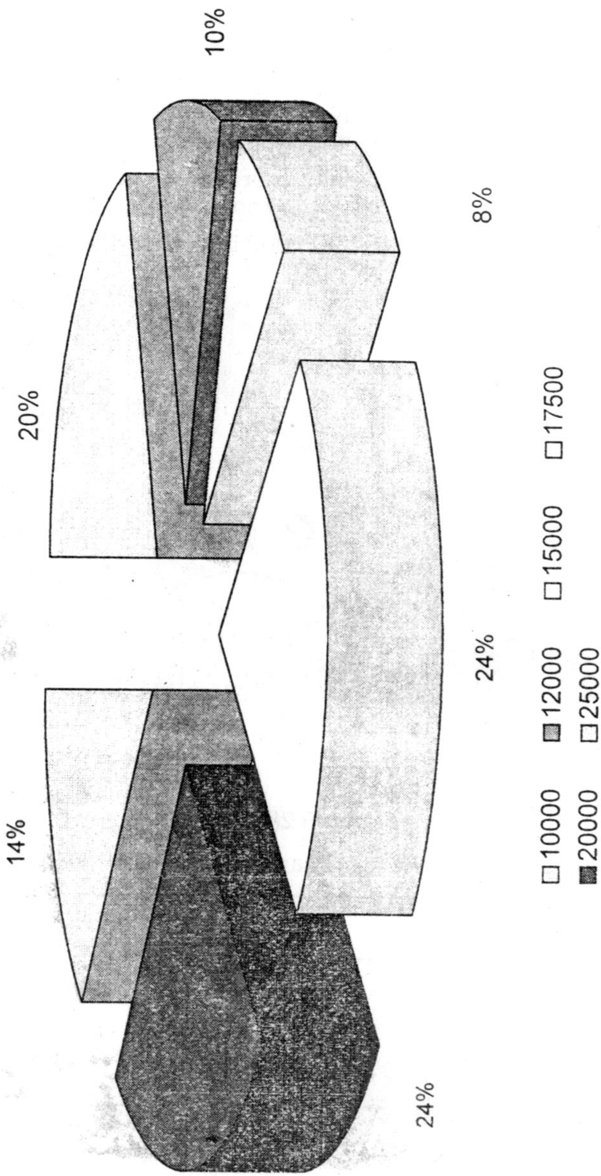
10%
20%
8%
14%
24%
24%
10000
12000
15000
17500
20000
25000

Impact on Digging Wells Activity

Out of 50 respondents, there were 24 loaners in the income range Rs.12,000 to Rs.17,500 in the pre-loan period and between in post-loan period also. On the other hand, there was a rise in the number of cases in the higher income levels i.e., from Rs.20,000 to Rs.27,500 in the post-loan provided as compared to pre-loan period. Average amount of income rose from Rs.15,127.27 to Rs.19,372.73 and Median income jumped up from Rs.15,000 to Rs20,000 in the post loan period.

Digging Wells

Table 5.28

Digging Wells Activity Loaners: Pre-loan Period

Sl. No	*Amount (Rs.)*	*Respondents*	*Per cent*
1.	12000	21	42.00
2.	15000	19	38.00
3.	17500	10	20.00
	Total	**50**	**100.00**

Average amount of increase in income: (Rs.) Mean: 15127.27 Median: 15000.

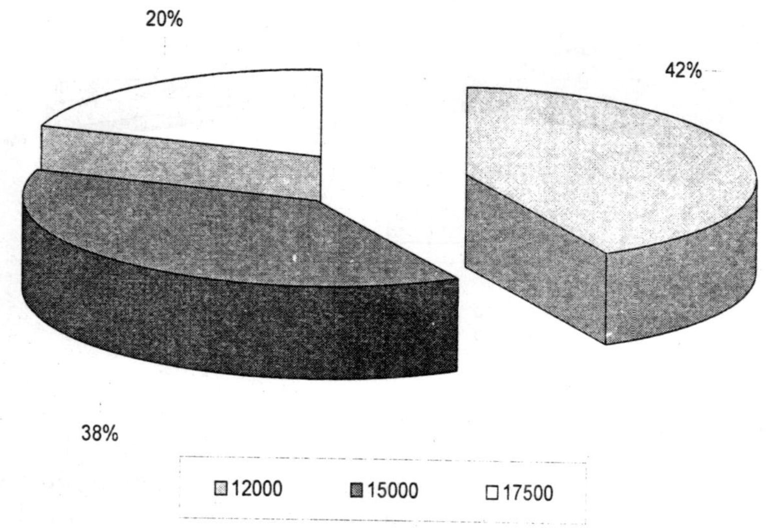

Digging Wells Activity Loaners: Post-loan Period

Sl. No	Amount(Rs)	Respondents	Per cent
1.	12000	14	28.00
2.	15000	3	6.00
3.	17500	7	14.00
4.	20000	10	20.00
5.	25000	11	22.00
6.	27500	5	10.00
	Total	**50**	**100.00**

Average amount of increase in income: (Rs.) Mean: 19372.73 Median: 20000.

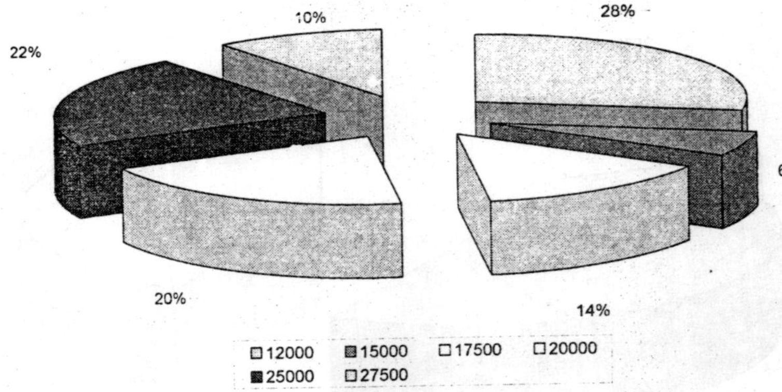

Impact of KCC on Farming Community

The changes that have taken place after obtaining KCCs by the beneficiary and their views are presented in the following table. The overall picture shows that there is significant impact on the farming community because of the KCCs. Majority of the respondents have expressed happiness over the performances of the KCCs and it has resulted in improving their standard of living. Also farmers have felt that better utilization of KCC has helped them to improve their socio-economic conditions. It is noteworthy that cent per cent of the farmers have changed their cropping pattern as this happened because of assured irrigation from the open well system. Another significant impact of the KCCs was that 49 per cent of the respondents took up some land improvement activities and 6 per cent of the farmers have adopted new technologies in their farms that to by the farmers belonged to medium and large category. Further to state that before KCCs, most of the farmers use to grow only non-commercial crops. But after the KCCs, majority of the farmers have used their credit to improve their existing open wells which has prompted to go in for cash crops. Change in cropping pattern has resulted in increasing of agricultural production and this was recorded in cases of 88 per cent respondents.

Table 5.29
Impact of the KCC on the Borrower's Household

Impact on the selected variables	*Category of the sample KCC beneficiary*				
	Marginal	*Small*	*Medium*	*Large*	*Overall*
Changes in cropping pattern	10 (100.0)	59 (100.0)	22 (100.0) (100.0)	9 (100.0)	100 (100.0)
Adoption of technologies	0 (0.0)	0 (0.0)	4 (18.2)	2 (22.2)	6 (6.0)
Improvement in the lands	4 (40.0)	27 (45.8)	12 (54.5)	6 (66.7)	49 (49.0)
In obtaining no-due certificate	8 (80.0)	52 (88.1)	19 (86.4)	9 (100.0)	88 (88.0)
Changes in household income level	7 (70.0)	47 (79.7)	20 (90.9)	8 (88.9)	82 (82.0)
Improvement in standard of living	9 (90.0)	55 (93.2)	21 (95.5)	8 (88.9)	93 (93.0)
Over all improvement of KCC beneficiary household	8 (80.0)	45 (76.3)	17 (77.3)	9 (100.0)	79 (79.0)

Note: Figures in parenthesis indicate per centage to total.

Opinion of the Non-KCC Farmers

To find the practical reasons for non-adoption of KCCs by these farmers, an opinion survey was carried out among 30 non-KCC farmers. Out of the selected 30 non-KCC holders, 10 farmers were belong to small farms followed by the same number from marginal farm and five each from medium and large farm respectively. The following result of the opinion survey was pertaining to 30 non-KCC farmers. From the table it can be inferred that the fear of repayment of loan is the highest in the case of all four categories of farmers. It is evident from the table that more than 50 per cent of the farmers (except large farm) responded that the fear of repayment is the factor which keeps them away from the institutional credit source. The farmers opined that the loan from the commission agents is repayable as the harvested produce makes its way to the market through commission agent and there is practice of deducting the loan amount from the sale proceeds of the agricultural produce. About 60 and 40 per cent of the farmers belongs to large and medium farmers respectively have not adopted KCC as they were satisfied with their own funds. Bad experience with institutional source of credit was resorted by 20 per cent farmers each belongs to small and marginal farms. Lack of awareness by the farmers regarding the benefits of institutional credit was recorded in 10 per cent cases each in the small and marginal farm category.

Table 5.30
Opinion of Non-KCC Farmers for non- Adoption of KCCs

Reasons	*Small*	*Marginal*	*Medium*	*Large*
Fear of repayment	50.00 (5)	60.00 (6)	60.00 (6)	40.00 (2)
Satisfied with own resources	20.00 (2)	20.00 (2)	40.00 (2)	60.00 (3)
Bad experience in the past with the institutional source of credit	20.00 (2)	20.00 (2)	0.00 (0)	0.0 (0)
Lack of awareness	10.00 (1)	10.00 (1)	0.00 (0)	0.00 (0)
Total	**100.00**	**100.00**	**100.00**	**100.00**

Source: Field Survey.

Efficacy of Kisan Credit Card Observation from Field

As a part of the study as many as 250 farmers who had availed the KCC facility were interviewed to ascertain their view points. The field visits had brought out several findings of importance, which could have a bearing on the future policy in their regard and also help in speeding up the progress of implementation by highlighting the operational difficulties. The feedback on the questionnaire which was administered to 250 KCC holders in a semi-structured interview has been presented in the following paragraphs.

Coverage of New Farmers

Out of the 250 farmers covered in the field study, 32 farmers were new borrowers. It may be quite possible that some of them were borrowing from other banks and may have shifted to new branches, but remaining 68 per cent were borrowers continuing with same banks. such a good number of new borrowers demanding Kisan Credit Card would be due to benefit associated with it and active involvement of commercial banks. Cooperatives RRBs along with the continuous monitoring of the progress by RBI and NABARD.

Adequacy of Credit

It may be mentioned here that Kisan Card Scheme envisaged coverage of all the short-term credit needs of the farmers including crop loan. Loan for maintenance of agricultural implements and machines like tractor, power tiller etc., advances to bear the maintenance cost of dairy units, cattle farming and loan for consumption expenditure to some extent. The idea behind this approach was to ensure that farmers get adequate credit to meet all of their short term needs through the single window of kisan card. As many as 53 farmers during field visit, felt that the credit limits sanctioned to them under Kisan Card were adequate. The rest 47 per cent which mostly comprised of borrowers belongs to areas of adequate irrigation felt that it was not adequate. Thus the borrowers having adequate irrigation generally want higher credit as compared to others. Further it has been mentioned. Kisan card also envisaged meeting the short-term credit need of the farmers for the purposes other than raising the crops cooperative banks had however not been providing such limits while sanctioning the credit limit to farmers under Kisan Card scheme. Commercial banks and RRBs had been sanctioning short-term credit for non-crop purposes regularly. There were not many complaints from cardholders of commercial banks and RRBs on the adequacy of credit under Kisan Card.

Facility of Drawal at Other Branches

One of the objectives of Kisan Card was to provide flexibility in operating upon the credit limit sanctioned to the borrower under the card. In tune with this spirit some of the commercial banks, albeit at a cost, had allowed their cardholders to draw cash from the branches other than the card issuing branch so that he could purchase inputs from the taluka or district headquarters and take the advantage of competitive prices of inputs.

Kisan Credit Card besides providing flexibility and adequate credit to meet all of the needs was also intended to reduce the cost of credit. Cardholder was expected to draw and repay as and when needed depending upon his cash flow. Frequent transactions would effectively reduce the outstanding loans thereby lowering the interest paid. About 46 per cent of farmers covered in 4 taluks, Mysore had frequent operations and utilized the Kisan Credit Card effectively. Whereas 54 per cent of the farmers did not make frequent operations on the limit sanctioned to them under the card. There could be many reasons for this. Firstly, many farmers were of the view that if they repay their loan before the due date, they would not get repeat loans. They were mostly guided by their previous experiences in this regard. Second factor, partly responsible for this was the complicated procedure of drawls based on the seasonal sub-limits of the total limit. This aspect need to re-examined carefully in the light of the fact that Kisan Card was aimed at to reduce the complications and simplify, the procedures so that farmers get greater access to bank credit. If the bank is sanctioning is revolving cash credit under Kisan Card for a period of 12 months, then the farmer should be permitted to operate upon it as freely as possible and in a very simple way some of the banks have followed this approach. Whereas few of the banks have complicated the procedure to such an extent that it has become a problem not only for the farmer but also to their field staff also to sanction the limit and monitor it. Thirdly, some of the farmers who had surplus amount but did not deposit it in the Kisan Card account were under the impression that they would not get any interest on credit balance. Their fears were mostly due to ignorance about the instructions in this regard as most of the banks had issued instruction to their branches to provide interest on the credit balance in the Kisan Card cash credit account. The protect of Kisan Credit Card practically is only 6 to 7 years old. It is expected that in another 5 years this would become a very popular financial product among the rural elements and farmers would use it very effectively. It is observed from the field study that in Mysore district all the farmers came to know about KCC only after year 2000.

End Use of Credit

During the field visit, an effort was make to ascertain the end use of credit for purposes for which the credit was sanctioned under the Kisan Card. There were apprehensions that in view of liberal approach adopted by banks regarding monitoring the end use like not insisting on documentary proofs of purchase of inputs etc., in the Kisan Card scheme, tendency to missutilize the credit would increase. The observations from the field however, indicate that most of farmers had used credit limit for their expanses on raising the crops, improvement of land increasing the area under irrigation and allied activities like dairy farming, etc. It is observed from field study that most of the farmers used credit only for agriculture purpose as they know very well their obligation of repaying debt in time. Some farmers had used a certain amount of sanctioned credit under KCC for consumption purposes also, as KCC had the provision of sanctioning some amount to meet the cash outflows on consumption expenses.

Purchase of Fertilizers and Other Inputs

The objective of the Kisan Credit Card scheme as given in the model scheme circulated by RBI and NABARD was to ensure adequate and timely support from banking system to farmers for their cultivation needs including purchase of inputs in a flexible and cost effective manner. The utility of Kisan Credit Card in purchase of fertilizers or other inputs was ascertained from the farmers during the field study. The Kisan Credit Card was extremely useful and it had many advantages over the earlier system of crop loaning. Firstly, there was no insistence by the banks on certain portion of limit to be lifted as kind component. Particularly by Commercial Banks and RRBs in most of the states and the farmer had the freedom to utilize the limit in the manner as suited to him. Secondly, there was no compulsion to buy inputs at the beginning of the cropping season. Farmer could buy the inputs during the off season, when these were cheaper. This helped in reducing cost of cultivation. Thirdly, the farmers were able to bargain over the prices of inputs from the dealer as they could pay in cash. They also had the freedom of selecting the shops/dealers unlike in the regular system of crop loans where choice of shops for purchase of inputs was limited. Fourthly, farmers could reduce some of the cost of inputs, as they did not have to pay commission to dealer to got bills and receipts as a documentary proof for purchase of inputs, which were necessary in the earlier system.

Cost of Kisan Credit Card-Service Charges

Generally banks have been levying various charges under

different names like service charges, folio charges, out of pocket expenses, penalty for lost listing of card, replacement of damaged card etc from the farmers for issuing kisan cards. These charges were highest among the commercial banks followed by RRBs and thereafter cooperative banks. But it was observed from field study that the concerned bank branches have not charged any fees on farmers for issuing KCC. In fact banks would be able to gain more and thus offset the additional cost of Kisan Credit Card by having more growth in business by attracting more farmers to avail kisan credit card facility.

Summary

This study revealed that, in 59.2 per cent cases, the amount of loan was found to be inadequate for the activity financed by the bank. The inadequacy of bank loan forced the loaners to borrow money from other sources. Out of total sample 42.80 per cent were found to be defaulters. In maximum cases of default, the loaners were willful defaulters.

The analysis of the impact of grameena bank credit on the income level of the farmers brought out that in 56 per cent cases the respondents were benefited by obtaining loan as it resulted in increase in the level of their income, in 44 per cent cases, the level of income of the respondents remained the same and no cases the income of the respondents fell from their pre-loan income. This indicates that the positive correlation of grameena bank credit and agricultural development in the district.

All the banks had issued detailed instruction, to their field functionaries on recovery of dues under the Kisan Credit Card scheme. Keeping in view the diversity in the agricultural practices, crops grown availability of irrigation facilities and cropping intensities and other complexities involved, many banks have given freedom to their branch managers in fixing the repayment schedules. In general, the credit limit sanctioned under the kisan credit is for a period of 12 months and each drawal is repayable within 12 months. In the field study it is observed that all farmers who availed KCC from Cauvery Grameena bank reported that the repayment of loan was on yearly basis while in case of Cauvery Grameena Bank, out of total 50 farmers interviewed, some 12 farmers said that they repay the loan on a half yearly basis.

Since the Kisan Credit Card was a innovative product there was a need to counsel and educate the farmers on the due dates in the new system so that farmers repay their dues in time. It was satisfying to know that all most all the farmers covered in the sample were aware of the repayment dates. Farmers were also aware of the benefits of timely repayment of dues.

6

Summary, Major Findings and Policy Implications

In the preceding chapters, a detailed field study analysis has been presented. On the basis of these chapters, in this chapter summary, major findings and policy implications have been presented. This chapter includes two parts. Part-I deals with major findings of the study, and part-II represents policy implications of the study.

Part I—Major Findings of the Study

Based on the analysis and discussion in the study of **"Regional Rural Banks and Agricultural Development - With Special Reference to Mysore District"**, the following findings have been drawn:

1. Over the last ten years or so, the Indian agriculture has witnessed shocks and changes. While the controls on imports of many agricultural products have been gradually removed due to obligations of World Trade Organisation, the growth of agricultural credit has also slowed down the nineties as compared to the eighties. Due to sharp decline in prices of many agricultural commodities, some farmers have

committed suicide. In the post-nationalization period, the commercial banks were directed to open large number of rural branches in hitherto unbanked centers. It is the major economic reforms of the 1990s, which gave an impetus to the rural credit delivery system of the commercial banks. There is no denial of the fact that scheduled commercial banks have picked up momentum especially in the post-economic reform period. This is indicative of the scheme emerging as a widely accepted mechanism for delivery of crop loans to farmers in a hastle free manner.

2. After about 70 years of constant efforts, institutional credit indeed reaching a substantial proportion of farmers. The significance of formal credit institutions in terms of credit delivery for the agricultural sector has increased over time. It is noteworthy that the share of cooperative credit institutions in total agricultural credit has declined in the last decade whereas the share of commercial banks and RRBs have increased during the same period. Therefore, the structural changes taking place in the Indian banking system after the financial sector reforms have worked against the agricultural sector. Major achievements have been made through Kisan Credit Scheme i.e., short-term loans.

   After the introduction of KCC scheme in 1998-99, so far a total of around six crores kisan credit cards have been issued covering all the major states of the country (till 2005). The number of KCCs issued accounts about 49 per cent of the total landholdings in the country. It is a remarkable progress over the past eight years.

3. In Karnataka about 23,09,000 kisan credit cards have been issued which accounts 6.3 per cent of the total for All India level (till 2004). In Mysore district, banks have issued Kisan Credit Cards to 48,454

farmers with a total credit at Rs. 216 crore (till September 2005).

4. It was found that the bank officials were keen to extend the facility of KCC to farmers. In most of the places, it is the bank personal who informed the farmers about the scheme and its benefits. All the respondent farmers indicated that obtaining KCC from banks is very easy. Further banks are not maintaining any minimum credit limit while issuing cards. Similarly the banks are not charging any fees on cardholders for obtaining KCC. Since the banks are not maintaining any minimum credit limit, the marginal and small cultivators who require small loans are not deprived of KCC facility.
5. An interesting point observed during the field study is that the majority of the farmers come under the category of small and marginal farmers. Prior to obtaining KCC most of the farmers used to borrow from indigenous village money-lenders as well as from primary agriculture cooperative credit societies. After introduction of KCC scheme there was a drastic decline in the importance of the village money-lenders in the village credit system. At the same time costs of borrowing from informal sources that is from money-lenders was also reduced.
6. Although the Kisan Credit Card scheme was introduced to the year 1998-99, it has become operational in the study area only from the year 2000 onwards. It was noticed that all most all the eligible farmers have obtained KCC cards. This is noteworthy.
7. Generally it is a know fact that education plays a major role in decision-making process. About 85% of the KCC holders in the study area are educated. Among the illiterate farmers, large chunk of them are found in small farm category. The level of education of the farmers is reflected in their

knowledge and ability of making use of credit for productive purposes. This has resulted in enhancing the agricultural productivity it as well as in increasing the total income of the households.

8. To meet the credit requirements of rural people in Mysore district, Cauvery Grameena Bank was established. Cauvery Grameena Bank has so far been able to achieve the objective of helping the weaker sections despite the constraints. Cauvery Grameena Bank within the reasonable limits has been doing its best to maximize the lendings to small entrepreneurs and persons engaged in service sector. The main objective of this bank has been to provide credit and other facilities especially to the small and marginal farmers, agricultural labourers, artisans and small entrepreneurs in rural areas. The numbers of accounts have also been increased rapidly.
9. Cauvery Grameena Bank also helps agriculture development by giving crop loans for meeting part costs of cultivation of crops repayable after the crops are raised and marketed.
10. Crop loans are advanced with the object of providing financial assistance to small and marginal farmers to purchase seeds. Chemical fertilizers and manure, pesticides, diesel and oil, to hire tractors, threshers and to pay wage the Labourers. This is production oriented loan and helps in raising the crop and thereby development of agriculture.
11. Cauvery Grameena Bank also contributes to agriculture development by giving loans to allied activities such as for purchase of bullocks and others.
12. Bank's credit operations are closely inter-linked with IRDP/SGSY programmes and allied programmes and thereby it is able to make significant contribution to rural development. Cauvery Grameena Bank's record in mobilisation of savings, disbursement of

advances as well as recovery of loans is impressive with its wide coverage in the district.

13. The cauvery grameena bank actively participated in implementing Government Sponsored poverty alleviation programmes. The bank assisted 75 groups under SGSY against a target of 73.
14. The bank has implemented the comprehensive packages for farmers as announced by Hon'ble Finance Minister and also initiated necessary action to agriculture sector. The total amount disbursed to agricultural sector is Rs. 132.93 crore against the target of Rs. 113.29 crore representing an achievement of 117.33%.
15. The bank has taken up promoting self-help groups during the year with the financial assistance of Rs. 4.30 lakh from NABARD as SHPI for promoting and linkage of 300 SHGs through 20 selected branches. The bank has formed/promoted 374 groups and credit linked 280 groups with an amount of Rs. 1.05 crore under the project.
16. The Women Development Cell conducted Gender Sensitization programme to selected staff of the bank. International Women's Day Celebration was also conducted at Head Office and also at Periyapatna, Nanjangud and T.Narasipura branches. This is need of the hour.
17. The average amount of post-loan income is substantially higher than pre-loan income for all the activities under study. In this sector, average pre-loan income is Rs. 4096.15, which has risen to Rs. 6144.23 in the post-loan period. There are 21 respondents with pre-loan income range between Rs. 3000 to Rs. 5000 who were not able to improve their income. There is one beneficiary in the income Rs. 5500 who is able to improve his income in post-loan period. The number of loaners in the income

ranges Rs. 6500 to Rs. 9000 is 30 in the post-loan period. There is increase in the number of respondents in the higher income levels in the post-loan period.

18. It has been observed during the course of the study that in cases of direct financing by banks for the purchase of two buffaloes giving a gap of six months of the beneficiaries were able to get a continuous flow of income, resulting in repayment of loans and better income effect on the beneficiary.

19. The dairy loans sponsored by animal husbandry department were found to have impressive effect on the income level of the beneficiaries. It is possible because of training imparted to the borrowers before sponsoring their cases to banks for providing loans. Some beneficiaries took up another allied to agriculture, namely piggery. By and large, the beneficiaries of this activity earned a good return because of low cost for running the activity.

20. When asked with farmers about the situation before availing of the KCC, majority of them have stated that their major area was under rain-fed conditions. As a result farmers were unable to earn good income from their agricultural activities. After availing KCC, initially most of the farmers in the study area spent their agricultural credit for enhancing area under irrigation. Of the total land of selected farmers, 45.83 per cent comes under dry/rainfed conditions. In this situation farmers should be appreciated for making use of credit in a productive manner to enhance area under irrigation facilities.

21. Before availing the KCC the selected farmers use to grow only low profile crops in the sense that they use to grow crops like paddy, cashew vegetables and other crops. Most of these crops were depended upon rainfall. After obtaining KCC most of them have utilized their credit amount to deepen/

construct well around open well/install diesel motors/electricity connection etc. This has resulted in assured irrigation which prompted them to go in for diversified crops in their farms. So, most of the farmers started changing their cropping pattern from traditional to commercial crops like aeronaut, coconut, rubber, pepper, etc., which they feel will fetch better income than traditional crops.

22. Nearly, 49 per cent of the KCC borrowers have availed the credit limit of Rs. 50,000 another 12 per cent are in the range of Rs. 50 to 75 thousands and the remaining farmers are in the ranges of Rs. 75,000 and above. It is found that in general there has been around 50 per cent increase in amount borrowed of the farm level after they were issued KCCs by all categories of farmer taken together. The extent of increase in amount borrowed at the farm level, after they were issued KCCs by all categories of farmers taken together. The extent of increase in amount borrowed by various categories of farmers varies from 46 per cent for small farmers, to 64 per cent in case of large farmers. As stated earlier, the amount borrowed form informal sources have come down by about 46 per cent in the combined sample. A fall in amount borrowed from informal sources was witnessed for all four categories of farmers without any exceptions.

23. After availing Kisan Credit Card, most of the farmers saw improvements in their total income. It was made possible due to timely availability of credit. It is noteworthy that as many as 85 per cent of the respondents were good enough in repaying loan. It shows that farmers have realized the importance of repayment and its revolving process. Similarly, 47 per cent of the respondents have used their total income to clear the old debt since it was causing unnecessary hardship for the beneficiaries.

Part II – Policy Implications

On the basis of our study, the following suggestions are recorded to make lending advances under priority and non-priority sector by the Cauvery Grameena Bank to the farmers to be more effective and purposeful:

1. It is important to note that most of the beneficiaries are illiterate. Hence, the beneficiaries need to be educated about the formalities to be fulfilled in obtaining the necessary finance. The bank staff should help of the uneducated farmers in getting their credit sanctioned from the banks. If the beneficiaries are educated they can get loans easily from the banks.
2. To reduce the problem of overdues, banks should announce certain incentives in the form of cash discounts etc. The farmers who have cleared the loan may be given rebate on interest and priority in giving loans by the bank. This would result in decreasing the number of defaulters in future.
3. The branches should provide credit assistance not only to their existing borrowers but also to other eligible persons within their command area provided they are not covered by any other financial agency. Immediate assistance would be needed for protecting and regenerating standing crops, repairs and protection of livestock sheds, for implements and for storage structure etc.
4. In addition to the general schemes to be adopted by all the RRBs specific area-wise schemes should also be formulated to suit the socio-economic conditions prevalent in the area of the Regional Rural Bank.
5. To avoid under interference of local leaders it is suggested that the local should not be permitted to act as intermediaries for the identification of

applicants or to pressurize the bank officials for sanctioning loans. They may be allowed to force the bank officials to permit loans to un-credit worthy applicants.

6. To reduce the time gap between the supply of credit and demand for credit, the credit should be given within short period. Apart from this, there is urgent need to streamline the procedures at branch-level and bank-level for the quick disposal of the loan applications.
7. The policy-maker should aim at securing the economic and political health of the people through agricultural credit. They should regard the principles of finance and accounting, but they should not be overemphasized. Agricultural credit is a matter which affects millions of people and in democracy, it is important that the people should also try to understand the rights and wrongs of borrowing matters which affect them. Their participation and opinion will shape the government policy.
8. Most of the banks are issuing cards to only those farmers who own agricultural land. Further of the important Basle's that farmers still face in borrowing from formal sources, the insistence on collateral seems to be the biggest one. The biggest challenge to the system, however is to reach those farmers who are not well off and cannot provide collateral security due to lack of assets.
9. The distribution of KCC as well as share in total credit disbursed through KCC was tilted in favour of small, medium and large farmers. However, the significant factor is that of adequate representation of small farmers in all the sample branches. At the same time, attention should be given to marginal farmers as well as SC/ST farmers.
10. Further, in the areas of adequate irrigation farmers

are not satisfied with actual credit limit fixed by the banks. They want more credit in order to make further improvements in agricultural land. The policy implication is that the credit limit should be enhanced in the areas of adequate irrigation.

11. During the field study, it was observed that personal accident insurance scheme was introduced by both Syndicate bank and Canara bank to its KCC holders.
12. The coverage under scheme should be extended in a manner such that financial institutions have to reach all existing borrowers who taken loan mainly from informal sources and those rule households who do not borrow. To maintain viability of KCC operations, the lending rates will have to be fixed in a manner which provide incentives to the borrowers for borrowing from formal institutions but do not threaten the long-term sustainability of the scheme. The way of estimating scale of finance being adopted by the various banks should be in accordance with changes in cropping pattern, technology, inputs use and availability of irrigation facility.
13. Hence, rigorous efforts have to be made by the bank officials to extend KCC to all farmers. It is necessary that the scope of KCC is expanded further to facilitate faster turnover the credit maintaining sustainability and long-term viability of the scheme is very important.
14. The KCCs aims at adequate and timely support from the banking system to the farmer to meet their credit needs of crop production and ancillary activities. As many as 73 per cent of the KCC beneficiaries were satisfied with the present cost of accessing the KCC limit, all the farmers were satisfied with the operational efficiency of the KCCs. The major constraints in the working of the KCCs were too

many intermediaries in obtaining the suitable securities and finding the guarantor. All the farmers were quite satisfied with the attitude of the loan officers.

15. Thus, by and large, the KCCs can be termed as quite efficient especially when it comes to the fulfillment of the short-term production credit requirements of all farm size classes. The credit gap on the small farm was modest and this could be bridged by the own funds to a substantial and reasonable extent. In the present study owned funds were not taken into account.

16. As for the further simplification of the procedure of extending credit under KCC, which still irks the beneficiaries, farmers can be issued a passbook with on authenticated record of the land and borrowing. The bank should accept the same as the valid title, for the purpose of the mortgage. This step will save the farmer from the cumbersome process of registering the mortgage deed in the name of the bank.

Bibliography

A Study for Assessing the Impact Rural Lending by Commercial Banks in Patiala District of Punjab State; State Bank of Patiala; Head Office. The Mall. Patiala; 1987 (Mimeo).

A.K.Tomar and Jaiprakash: *Role of Regional Rural Banks in Economic Development,* Mohit Publications, New Delhi.

Agarwal, R.B.L.: "Concessional Finance — Do Weaker Sections benefit?". *Economic Times,* August, 16,1982), P.5.

Agarwal, R.K.: Evaluation of the Working of Regional Rural Banks. Mittal Publications, New Delhi, 1991.

Agarwal, R.N.: *Rural Banking in India,* Oxford and I.B.H Publishers, New Delhi.

Alak Ghosh; Role of Regional Rural Banks. *The Economic Studies,* Vol.17, No.1, July, 1976.

Angadi, V.B. "Banks" Advances to priority sectors—an enquiry into the causes of concentration", *Economic and Political Weekly,* Vol. XXVIII, No. 13, (March 26, 1983).

Batra, J.D.: *Rural Banks for the Rural Poor.* Kurukshetra, 26 (2), 16 October, 1977.

Bhatnagar, R.C. "Recovery of Agricultural Loans". *State Banks of India Monthly Review,* Vol. XXI, No.2, (Feb. 1982), pp. 43-48.

Bhatnagar, R.C.: "Recovery of Agricultural Loans".*State Banks of India Monthly Review*, Vol. XXI, No.2, (Feb. 1982), pp. 43-48.

Biswajit Chatterji and Amit Kundu (2001): "Rural Banks in India's Agrarian Economy - New Agenda for Reforms", Deep and Deep Publications, New Delhi.

Bose, A.: "Commercial Banks and Rural Finance" *State Bank of India monthly Review*, Vol. XXI, No.6, (June, 1982), pp. 211-16.

Chatterji Biswajit and Amit Kundu (1999) " Rethinking Rural Financial Institution", paper presented in the 35th Annual Conference of the Indian Economic Society at Jaipur, March-1999.

Das, Tushar, K., "Agricultural Financing by Commercial Banks", *Commerce, Pamphlet*, No.99 (March, 1976).

Deshande D.V., Mudgal M.K., Gupta, K.K (1996): Regional Rural Bank at Cross Roads, Bankers Institute of Rural Development, Lucknow.

Dhabatosh Dutta: Planning for Rural Banks. *Economic and Political Weekly*, Vol.11,No.25, August 27th, 1977.

Evaluation and Monitoring Cell: Economic Research Department of State Bank of India; "Impact of Bank Credit on Weaker Sections in Kerala" *State Bank of India Monthly Review*, Vol. XXVI, No. 9, Sep. 1987, pp. 444-58.

G.S. Monga and R.K.Sinha (2001): "Nationalization of Banks-Retrospect and Prospects", Deep and Deep Publications Pvt.Ltd. New Delhi.

Ganesan, P. (1996): A Study of Priority Sector Advances.vis-à-vis Profits and Profitability of Public Sector Banks in India: 1969-1993 (an unpublished Ph.D. thesis) Bharathiar University, Coimbatore, T.N.

Ganguti, A.K: *Rural Banking*, Margin, Vol. 9. No. 2, January, 1977.

Ghiara, B.M.: "Agricultural Financing by Commercial Banks-A look ahead", *PRAJNAN*, Vol. VI, No.3 (Jul-Sept. 1977), pp. 261-305.

Ghosal, S.N. (1998): *Agricultural Financing in India,* Asia Publishing House, Bombay.

Gian Kar (2001): "Nationalisation of Banks and Agricultural Credit in India", Deep and Deep Publications, New Delhi.

Hirannaiah, B. (2003): "An Analysis on the adoption of new farm technology in Cauvey Basin of Karnataka" Ph.D thesis submitted to University of Mysore, unpublished.

Jagdish Prasad and Sunil Kumar: Role of Regional Rural Banks. Kurukshetra , Vol.XXXIII, No. 14, May,1985.

Jain, Inu. "Rural Credit and Regional Rural Banks", Khadi Gramodyog, December 1980.

Kalkundrikar A.B. (1990): *Regional Rural Banks and Economic Development,* Daya Publishing House, Delhi.

Kashalikar, U.M.: "Problems of Overdue in the Nationalized Banks: A Case Study," Journal of Shivaji University; Vol.24, 1986-87.

Krishna.G., (1990): "Service Area Approach: Some Neglected Aspects", *Proceedings and Papers of Bank Economists Conference-1990* (Bombay, Himalaya Publishing House).

Krishnaswamy, K.S., (1980): "Priority Sector Lending and the 20-point Economic Programme : Role of Banks", Reserve Bank of India, p. 18.

Kumar Sunil (1990): RRBs and Rural Development, Deep and Deep Publications, New Delhi.

Kumud Sharma, *Co-operative V/s Commercial Bank Finance To Agriculture,* A Thesis Submitted to Karnatak University (1977).

Kurulkar, R.P. (1997): *Agricultural Finance in a Backward Region,* D.K. Publishers and Distributors, New Delhi.

Lal, R.C. and Lavania, R. F.: *Impact of Credit on Agricultural Production and Income,* Indian Co-operative Review 1986 23(3).

Leelabai, S.N.: *Agricultural Finance in Underdeveloped Economies-*

with Special Reference to India, A Thesis Submitted to Bombay University for Ph.D Degree.

M. C. Agarwal: *Farm Level Benefits and Costs of Agricultural Production,* Indian Journal of Agricultural Economics Oct-Dec. 1993, No. 4.

M.D.Dodke and D.B. Kudhatiya, *Short-term Credit Gap and Credit Requirements for Different Category of Farmers in Junagadh District,* Indian Co-operative Review, vol. XXXVI, No. 2, October 1998.

Mahendra, D. Desai and Bharat, D. Naik: *Prospect of Demand for Short-term Institutional Credit for HYV,* Indian Journal of Agricultural Economics, Vol. XXVI, No. 4 Oct. - Dec. 1971.

Mans, P. Binshanger and Mark R. Rosenweig: *Credit Markets, Wealth and Endowments in Rural South India,* VIII World Economic Congress Conference, Vol. No. 14, New Delhi.

Mathur B.L (1989): *Indian banking – Performance, Problems and Challenges,* National Publishing House, Jaipur.

Meenakhsi Rajeev and Sharmistha Dev: *Institutional and Non-Institutional Credit in Agriculture- Case Study of Hugli District of West Bengal,* EPW Nov. 21, 1998.

Mehta, G.S. (2001): *Prospects of Development,* Indus Publishing Company, New Delhi.

Mohiddin, K.S.S.Vduman (1991): *Institutional Credit and Agricultural Development,* Mittal Publications, New Delhi.

M.M.Vaggannavar, *Overdues in Primary Agricultural Credit Co-operatives in Karnataka",* Ph.D. Thesis submitted to Karnatak University, 1990.

Mukherjee,P.: *Banks and Rural Development.* Khadi Gramodyog, 23 (3), 1976.

Murti. T.V., Vashist, G.D and Parmar, U: *Utilization and Overdues of Co-operative Loans in Himachal Pradesh,* Indian Co-operative Review 26 (1) 1988.

Muthuswammy, Gopalan and Balakrishna B: *Credit*

Delinquency in Agricultural Co-operatives, Tamil Nadu Journal of Co-operation, Vol. 73, No. 3, 1987, NABARD reports various issues.

Nagabhushana Rao, E. and Krishna Murthy, B: Five Years of Regional Rural Banks. Kurukshetra, Vol. XXIX No. 8. January 16, 1981.

Naidu, L.K. (1998): *Bank Finance for Rural Development,* Ashish Publishing House, New Delhi.

Naidu M.R. and Prasad, J.V.S.: *Utilization Pattern and Productivity of Cooperative Production Credit,* Indian Cooperative Review, July 1987.

Nakkiran, S. (1996): *Agricultural Financing and Rural Banking in India,* D.K. Publishers and Distributors, New Delhi.

Nanavati Mahilal. B. and Anjaria, J.J.: *The Indian Rural Problem,* The Indian Society of Agricultural Economics, Bombay, 1960.

Naqi Uddin (2003): *Regional Rural Banks and Development,* A Mittal Publication, New Delhi.

Narasimham Committee; Report of the Committee on the Financial System: Reserve Bank of India Bulletin; Vol. XLVI, No. 2, Feb. 1992, pp. 369-80.

Naresh Kumar: How Banks help in Rural Development. Kurukshetra, 30 (17), 1 June,1982.

Naresh Kumar: Regional Rural Banks Helps Rural Development. The Maharashtra Co-operative Quarterly, Vol. IXVI. No. 2, October, 1982.

Narula R.K (1999): *Agricultural and Rural Advances by Commercial Banks – Practical Guidelines,* D.K. Publishers and Distributors, New Delhi.

Natarajan, B.: *Regional Rural Banks for Integrating Rural Development.* Swarajya, 21(7), August 1981.

Negi, Bhupal Singh (1990): *Cooperative Credit and Regional Development,* Deep and Deep Publications, New Delhi.

Pai Panandivar, V.A.: *Regional Rural Banks. Economic Times* (Supplement), 26 June, 1982.

Panda R.K. (1997): *Agricultural Indebtedness and Institutional Finance,* Ashish Publishing House, New Delhi.

Pandey Raj Kishore (1969): *Institutional Credit for Agriculture in India,* Ashish Publishing House, New Delhi.

Patel & Shete: Some Aspects of Recovery of Loans of Weaker Sections under Priority Sector Lending, *Prajanan,* Vol. XIII, No.1 (Jan-March 1984).

Pradesh Wadhwa, CD, Rural Banks for Rural Development, (New Delhi: the Machmillan Company of Indian Ltd. 1980).

Rajeev, Meenakshi and Sharmistha Deb (1998): "Institutional and Non-Institutional Credit in Agriculture", Serials Publications, New Delhi.

Rama Krishna, K. (1994): *Financing Institutional and Regional Development in India,* Chugh Publication, Allahabad.

Ramachandra Rao, (1995): *All about Priority Sector Advances.* Suneja publishers, New Delhi.

Raman Murthy, D.V: *Regional Rural Bank – An Assessment of Performance.* Southern Economist, 16(7),1 August,1977.

Ratanlal Gupta: *What Rural Banks Need to do? The Economic Studies,* Vol. 16, No. 34, September- October 1975.

Rayudu C.S. (1991): *Rural Credit in India,* Mittal Publications, New Delhi.

Rayudu, C.S.: C.N. Krishna Naik: *Management of Rural Banking;* Deep and Deep Publications, New Delhi, 1991, p. 175.

Reports

Report of All Indian Rural Credit Review Committee, Chairman, D.Venkatappaiah, Bombay, 1969.

Report of the Review Committee on Regional Rural Banks, Dantwala Committee, Bombay, 1977.

Report on Trend and Progress of Banking in India, 1989-90, Reserve Bank of India, p. 421.

Reserve Bank of India : Regional Rural Banks Act of 1976.

Sharada, H.M.: Study of the Regional Rural Banks. Lok Udyog, 14(3), June, 1980.

Sharma, K.K : Role of Regional Rural Banks. Southern Economist, 14(21), March 1, 1976.

Siddaiah, T. (1984): Social Banking in Chittoor District, Ph.D thesis submitted to Sri Venkateshwara University, Tirupati.

Sivachithappa, K.: Regional Rural Banks and Priority Sector Lending, Chethana Book House, Mysore (2004).

Srivastava,R.N: Impact of Champaram Kshetriya Grameena Bank of Rural Economy. Economic Affairs, Vol. 26, No. 1, 1981.

Subba Rao, K. : Credit to farmers who benefits. Kurukshetra. Vol. XXVII, No. 1, October, 1979.

Suneja, H.R., (1982): Bank Lending to Priority Sector, Concept Publishing House, New Delhi.

Thingalaya, N.K.: The Regional Rural Banks and Agriculture, Commerce, 139 (3577) 1979.

Thingalaya N.K., (2006) Karnataka. Fifty years of Banking Development, Justice K.S. Hegde Institute of Management, Nitte, Karnataka.

Tripathi,S.D: Integrated approach to Rural Banking. Eastern Economist, Vol. 65, No.8, 1976.

V.S. Bhat: *An Enquiry into the Working of Multipurpose Service Co-operative Societies in Sirsi Taluka, Karnataka State with special Reference to Totgar Co-operative Sale Society in Sirsi* (1993), thesis submitted to Karnatak University.

Varshneya J.S.: "Regional Rural Banks", *Khadi Gramodyog,* December 1980.

Vasan Anand Kumar: Performance of Regional Rural Banks, Kurukshetra, Vol. XXXVI, No. 8, May, 1988.

Velayudham, T.K. and Sankaranarayanan : Regional Rural Banks and Rural Credit . Economic and Political Weekly, September, 22,1990.

Venkiteswaran, S. (1984): *Performance of Co-operative Banks in Kerala - A Study on the Operational Efficiency of Primary Agricultural Credit Societies,* Ph.D. thesis, University of Kerala, Trivandrum.

Wadhya, C.D.: Rural Banks for Rural Development, Macmillian, Delhi, 1989.

Index